Petfinder.com

Presents:

SECOND CHANCES

Inspiring Stories of Dog Adoption

Joan Banks

Introduction by Betsy Saul, cofounder and president of Petfinder.com

Adams Media
Avon, Massachuset

*This book is dedicated to all of the selfless people who work in
animal welfare and to the hundreds of thousands of wonderful
dogs annually who don't find "forever" homes.*

Published by
Adams Media, an F+W Publications Company
57 Littlefield Street
Avon, MA 02322
www.adamsmedia.com

ISBN 10: 1-59337-660-X
ISBN 13: 978-1-59337-660-4

Printed in the United States of America.

J I H G F E D C B A

Library of Congress Cataloging-in-Publication Data
Banks, Joan
Petfinder.com presents : second chances / by Joan Banks ;
introduction by Betsy Saul.
p.   cm.
ISBN 1-59337-660-X
1. Dogs—United States—Anecdotes. 2. Dog adoption—United States—
Anecdotes. 3. Dog owners—United States—Anecdotes. 4. Petfinder.com (Firm)
I. Petfinder.com (Firm) II. Title.
SF426.2.B36 2006
636.7—dc22
2006014729

Photos provided courtesy of dog owners.

*This book is available at quantity discounts for bulk purchases.
For information, please call 1-800-872-5627.*

Contents

Introduction v

The Puppy Mill Dog. 1

A Dill-y of a Dog 6

Gone to the Dogs. 11

Turn about Is Fair Play. 16

Neighborhood Watchdog. 20

The Play's the Thing 24

A Smilin' Pit Bull. 28

A Sign of Love 33

Teacher's Pet. 38

Mister Lucky. 43

Finding Carrie 47

Everybody Needs a Buddy 52

Going to Kansas City. 55

Many Hands, Many Hearts 61

The House That Jake Built 65

A Labradoodle To-Do 69

Sentimental Journeys 74

Traveling Life's Roads. 78

Full House 82

Happiness Is a Big Bouvador 86

Blessed Events 92

Going the Distance 95

Tammy's Hero. 99

From 238 to No. 1 103

Home Again. 107

Poodle Fever. 112

Gentle Guardian. 117

In the Nick of Time 122

Quite a Dandy 127

Called to Service 132

The Wisdom of a Sage 137

A Friend Indeed. 141

A Helping Paw 145

Out of Stir 150

It's a Miracle. 154

Every Wish Way But Loose 158

The Detect-o Dog 163

Love at First Byte 167

Family Relations. 171

One of the Family 175

Hank the Cow Dog To-Be 179

A Very Special Boo Boo. 182

Hello Dolly! 187

On the Job 192

Orlando and Dawn 196

That's Scamp 201

A Long Way Home 205

Fitting In 209

A Fetching Fellow 214

Problem Pet to Perfect 218

On the Road Again 223

A Comforting Canine 227

Melorah's Special Assistant 232

The Sweetness of Being 238

For the Love of a Schnauzer. .243

Gift of Life 246

Introduction

A second chance for every homeless pet is just what my husband, Jared, and I had in mind when we created Petfinder.com in 1996. It seemed clear that if we could harness the infant technology of the Internet, we could bring critical attention to millions of pets that were dying simply because they had nowhere to call home.

It worked. Today, there are hundreds of thousands of pets posted on the Web site. Potential adopters, from their own homes, enter information into their computers about what type of pets they are looking for. They are rewarded with a list of potential new best friends from shelters and adoption groups all across the country and beyond. For the pets, this second chance is all they need. Each year, more than a million pets find their forever homes by being listed on Petfinder.com.

Over the years, thousands of adopters have sent us their stories. More often than not, people describe how they saw a particular pet online and, "it was love at first sight." They might have browsed through dozens of photos. Other times, it was the first to pop up on their monitor after they entered their search criteria, but when they saw it, stars sparkled and fairy dust fell. That special pet was not always at the local shelter. Sometimes, he or she was halfway across the country. But when people felt the magic, they didn't let distance stand in the way.

I hope you enjoy the stories of these special pets. We created Petfinder.com to save homeless pets, but what we learned is that often the pets we love save us.

—BETSY SAUL, COFOUNDER AND PRESIDENT OF PETFINDER.COM

The Puppy Mill Dog

Two women approached the brick ranch-style house along a tree-lined drive in rural Missouri. Nothing about the tidy acreage hinted that it was a puppy mill and that in the barn behind the house dogs were being kept under deplorable conditions.

The owners showed the women into their comfortable family room, which served as the selling area. Photos of dogs lined the walls. Most folks who wanted to buy a puppy stopped here; they never went out back. If they had, they might have changed their minds about purchasing a $700 pooch from these people.

But the two visitors today weren't there to buy puppies. They were there to rescue four mature females destined to be shot because they were of no more value to the owners.

"The only thing I can give these people credit for is that at least they give us a chance to rescue animals that are no longer breedable," says Debi Baker, founder of Recycled Rovers of Morse Mill, Missouri, who was there that day.

The owners escorted the two women to the barn that housed four hundred dogs, each of whom produced about two litters a year. The dogs lived in two-by-two-foot wire cages, stacked and suspended above a concrete slab.

A four-year-old black-and-white Shih Tzu shrank down on the wire floor as the four stopped in front of her cage and opened the door. Usually humans approached to take her out for breeding or to rip her puppies from her. This time, gentle hands reached in. A human stroked her and spoke softly. This was something new.

But new things scared her. Like her mother before her, she had little experience outside of a cage. The Shih Tzu's coat had none of the silky beauty typical of her breed. Dermatitis had caused much of her hair to fall out. What was left clumped in mats. Infections covered her skin and her eyes were milky. Overgrown toenails curled back into the pads of her paws.

She was one of four dogs that the women rescued that day.

Back at her place, Debi Baker named the little dog *Betty* and began to clean her up. She shaved away the mats of hair and bathed her. Betty took the grooming quietly and calmly, though it was a brand new experience.

"I've never seen a dog from a mill that was aggressive," Debi says. "Physically bad, yes; battered and scarred, yes; but mean? Never."

A veterinarian put the pooch on a regimen of antibiotics to try to save her eyes and her abscessed teeth and to cure her infections.

Meanwhile a question loomed: *Now that she had been saved from certain death, who would want to adopt such a pitiful dog?*

Debi had faith. She posted Betty's photo and description on Petfinder.com. "When I looked into Betty's eyes, there was something there that touched me," Debi says. "I knew someone else would see it too."

That someone else turned out to be Maggie Winegarden of Iowa City, Iowa. The Winegardens, David and Maggie and the two of their five sons who were still at home, had a mature springer spaniel, but they knew Bo, at twelve years old, wouldn't be with them many more years. They wanted to introduce a new dog into their home before they suffered the loss of Bo.

Maggie wanted a small dog that her youngest son, Nate, could manage, and who would sit in his lap. When she learned about Shih Tzus from a friend who had one, she decided the breed would be a good choice. She had begun searching regularly on Petfinder. com, and when Debi posted Betty, she popped up on Maggie's next search.

"My heart went out to her," Maggie says. She told her husband about the dog, and the two of them drove to Missouri to meet her. Though Debi had tried to prepare them, they were still shocked when they saw Betty.

"Oh, no," Maggie thought to herself. "A *wasted trip.*"

Nevertheless, they spent some time with Betty, and Maggie held the pooch in her lap and petted and talked to her.

Finally, Maggie stood up and told Debi, "My husband and I need to go somewhere and talk about this."

Debi understood. Taking on a dog like Betty was a serious commitment, and she didn't want an adoption failure.

"David and I found a coffee shop," Maggie says, "and sat down and just looked at each other. 'Do you think we can handle this?' I asked him."

David was skeptical.

Maggie was thinking aloud as she talked. "You know, this isn't for us; this is for her. When I sat there, holding her in my lap, she looked at me with those hazy eyes and seemed to say, 'I know you're going to help me.' I think we owe it to her. Look at what people have done to her."

David said he would support Maggie no matter what. He admitted that if he were there alone, he probably wouldn't adopt Betty, but if Maggie wanted the dog, that was okay with him.

Maggie's decision was to adopt. "I think Debi was surprised when we came back," Maggie says. "She probably thought she'd never see us again."

Back in Iowa City, Betty's treatment and rehabilitation continued. The antibiotics did their job. Her eyes, though damaged from being untreated for so long, cleared up. Maggie worked on her grooming. "I would brush her with a soft baby brush and get these mounds of white flaky dandruff flying off her skin."

Betty had missed most of a puppy's early learning experiences and exercise while she was caged. She now had to make up for lost time. Climbing the stairs in the Winegardens' home was a big hurdle. Maggie helped by moving one of Betty's paws to the next tread, and then Betty would simply wait, lacking the self-confidence to make a move. "One paw at a time" proved to be their motto for the next few weeks.

Something as simple as going on a walk was a new experience, so at first Maggie would carry her around the yard. "I had to get her used to being outside."

Her socialization was also stunted. Though Betty bonded to Maggie like glue, when others approached her, she shied away. With time, tender loving care, and judiciously administered treats, Betty became more trusting and would sometimes let people come up to her without backing away.

She was so incredibly docile and relaxed when placed in someone's lap that several people told Maggie she would make a good therapy dog. Maggie signed her up for the certification test, and she passed on the first try. The little dog who had spent her first four years with no loving attention was now fussed over and petted as she brought comfort to people in hospitals.

Puppy millers robbed Betty of a puppy's joy and exuberance; they stole her health. Those things could never be returned. But thanks to several remarkable people and a connection made by Petfinder.com, Betty would live out the rest of her days in a loving home.

A Dill-y of a Dog

Lisa Dill's year started badly when her father passed away after a short illness. Several months later, Lisa herself had to have surgery. What she thought would be an overnight stay turned into four days. Next, she arrived home to find Toby, the family's Border collie, acting strange.

"At first I just thought he had been missing me," she says. "But then he didn't get better. One evening I took him out, and he could hardly walk. I could hear his bones crunching with each step."

The next morning she took him to the veterinarian, who diagnosed Toby with a bone disease.

"The vet told me that my dog was not going to get any better," Lisa recalls, "and the best thing I could do for him was put him down. I couldn't believe what I was hearing. My friend of fifteen years needed me to make the decision to let him go on to a better place, free of pain and sickness. I didn't want to see him suffer anymore, so I watched as my little dog slipped away from me forever."

Lisa fretted about breaking the news to her family. "They all thought Toby was coming home with me and would get better. They had just lost their grandpa, who had lived nearby, and now this."

Lisa realized there was one way she could protect herself from further heartbreak.

"I'll never get another dog," she thought. That was October.

The following February, Lisa's cousin, Kelli Berezin from Austin, dropped in to visit unexpectedly. After the initial hellos, she booted up her laptop computer to show the Dills photos of her five dogs.

"While Lisa was looking at the pictures, I could sense that she really missed having a dog," Kelli says.

She was absolutely right. Not only was Lisa charmed by the dogs' photos, but the looks on the faces of her husband and boys made her realize she couldn't deprive her family of a canine companion.

That night, she logged onto Petfinder.com and began to search for a pet to adopt. She entered her search criteria, pressed *Enter*, and scanned the first nineteen pets that the site listed. She felt nothing.

Then Lisa looked at number twenty. His name was Merlin, and he was at Evansville Animal Care and Control in Evansville, Indiana.

She called her three boys to come and take a look at the tan and black fuzzy pup with the floppy ears and merled back. The back part was obviously Australian shepherd, but the front part was anyone's guess. The kids were just as excited as their mom, and they went so far as to give him a new name that they thought better suited him: *Ozzy*. As they read about him, however, their excitement turned to worry.

"It said that this little guy was scheduled to be put down on Monday morning," Lisa recalls. "This was on Sunday night."

The next morning, Lisa started calling the shelter at 5:00 A.M. because she didn't know when it opened and at what time they euthanized. After two and a half nerve-wracking hours, someone answered, and Lisa asked about Merlin.

"I'm sorry," the voice over the phone said. "We don't have him anymore."

Lisa immediately thought the worst, but then the staffer continued. "Merlin has gone to a foster home."

In fact, Jamie Weber, a volunteer at Evansville Animal Care and Control, had pulled Merlin from the shelter a week earlier, but the staff had not noted the transfer on his Petfinder.com listing. Jamie had not gone to the shelter to find a pup to foster. In fact, "No more dogs" was her mantra because she had trouble giving them up once she got them home. She had pooches at home to prove it, and her husband had drawn the line at four. She was there that day for a cat, a ferret, or a rabbit.

On that particular afternoon, she had walked by Merlin's cage, and the star on his information card jumped out at her. It meant he was scheduled for euthanasia on the following Monday morning.

Jamie did some quick calculations. Animal Care and Control had found Merlin wandering the streets. No owners had come looking for him, and now it was Saturday afternoon—the end of his seventh day. Tomorrow Merlin would be available for adoption.

The timing shattered Jamie. The shelter was closed on Sunday, Merlin's adoption day, and he would be euthanized on Monday morning before the shelter opened.

"In essence," Jamie says, "he was getting zero adoption time."

It was unacceptable to her. Jamie took Merlin's card to the office and arranged to take him home with her, mantra or not.

Lisa Dill got Jamie's number from the shelter and called to ask about Merlin. Lisa's heart almost stopped again when Jamie acted puzzled. Seconds ticked by before Jamie recalled that she had changed the dog's name.

"We renamed him Ozzy," Jamie said.

Goose bumps jumped out on Lisa's arms. Jamie had chosen the name the Dills had picked out for him.

Jamie told her that Ozzy had kennel cough, but that didn't stop Lisa from going to meet him. What she found at that meeting was a sick little guy who wasn't acting much like a puppy.

"He was weak and sluggish," she says, "but I knew in my heart he was the dog for us. I asked her if I could bring my kids back after school to meet him."

Later that day, she returned with the children. It only took them a few minutes, and they knew, too. Ozzy was adopted that night—Valentine's Day.

Jamie wanted to keep Ozzy awhile longer to continue his treatments for kennel cough, and the Dills agreed. Greg Dill, who was seventeen at the time, called several times a day to check on the pup.

"I think Jamie finally got tired of all the calls," Lisa says with a laugh, "so she said we could come and get him."

Ozzy came to his new home, and for the first time in many months, the Dills' house was full of joy. Ozzy loved playing in the big backyard, and walks were special treats.

When the Dills took Ozzy for a checkup, they asked the vet to estimate how old he was so they could pick a day to celebrate his birthday. The vet said he was probably born in the middle of October.

"How about October fifteenth?" Greg asked.

A chill ran up Lisa's spine. "What they didn't realize was that October fifteenth was my dad's birthday. If he had met Ozzy he would have fallen deeply in love with him, just the same as we have."

Ozzy's adoption broke a streak of bad luck for the Dills, and for Ozzy it meant a life brimming with love.

Gone to the Dogs

Before Ken Foster met Duque, he scoffed at the whole "dog thing," as he called it. A writer, he was at an artists' colony in Costa Rica when the small tan mutt started following him back to his apartment each day after lunch. "He would take a nap for about an hour, then leave. Next Duque started showing up at dinner time, then in the morning."

Ken took this attachment very personally and quickly became quite fond of the little guy. When his stay at the colony ended, Ken wanted to bring Duque back to the States with him. As it turned out, airline restrictions wouldn't allow it. Meanwhile, he found out he wasn't the only one who felt singled out by what appeared to be Duque's allegiance.

"I thought it was all about me," Ken recalls, "but I discovered Duque had a schedule. He spent the morning with the gardener and someone else in the afternoon." Everyone sort of thought Duque was theirs. Had Ken managed to adopt him, a whole raft of people probably would have been upset when he took off with *their* dog.

Duque-less, he returned to New York City, but Ken had already begun his transformation into a dog person and was intent on adopting one.

He saw a mention of Petfinder.com in the *New York Post*, so he logged on and began searching. One dog that caught Ken's eye was Brando, a male puppy at BARC (Brooklyn Animal Resources Coalition). Even though he had planned to adopt an older dog, something about the little brindle pup appealed to Ken.

Ken called the shelter to find out more about him. The staff wasn't sure Brando was there anymore because the dogs were temporarily housed in another location while a new facility was being built.

"I decided to take the train over to check out what they had," Ken remembers. "It was in the middle of winter, there was snow everywhere, and I had just gotten back from living in Central America. I arrived at this temporary shelter, which was an old warehouse, and it was very depressing. The dogs were in this one big room, and all of them started barking and yapping and leaping in the air, and I thought, *'I'm not going to take one of these dogs; they're crazy.'* But then I saw this one dog that was just sitting and staring at me. I looked up and read his information card. It was Brando."

Ken didn't want to leap into pet ownership too quickly, so every day he went to walk Brando and get acquainted. "Brando was so uncertain of things that he didn't want to go any further than the sidewalk outside the shelter," Ken says. "I carried him to a nearby park to play." At the end of each visit, the puppy seemed relieved to be back at the shelter.

On the fourth day, they followed the same scenario, but when they reached the shelter door, the puppy looked up at Ken, his eyes asking, "Do you *really* want me to go back there?"

Ken was still hedging, but he worried constantly that Brando would be adopted in his absence. "I'd tell the staff, 'I want to adopt him, so don't let anyone else take him, but I want to visit a few more times.' The staff was great about it. They said, 'Yeah, go ahead; it's better to make sure.'"

He went out of town for a few days and when he returned, he hurried out to the shelter. "They have these volunteer dog walkers, and as I turned the corner I saw Brando on a leash about to go on a walk with someone. Brando saw me, too, and started getting excited." Feeling very possessive, Ken ran up to the volunteer and said, "That's my dog. I'll take him now."

Ken adopted Brando that morning and called a car service to take them to Manhattan. "He licked my face the whole way home."

Ken's life was changed. Instead of watching television in the morning, he walked Brando to a dog run several blocks from their apartment where Ken read the paper while Brando played. Along the way, they met neighbors Ken had never spoken to who were out with their canine companions.

Ken had considered whether having a dog in the city was a good idea, but he soon realized there was a whole dog culture (the name, incidentally, of a book he later edited) that he was unaware of before he adopted Brando.

"The really great thing about having a dog in the city is that you meet all sorts of people you wouldn't otherwise encounter," he says. "I met doctors and lawyers and students, whereas before I only knew writers."

Brando suffered from separation anxiety, so Ken found himself staying home more—resulting in more time to work on his novel—and the dog was always a good excuse to get home. Ken's weight dropped from all the exercise he was getting on three walks a day, and he and Brando got involved in charitable activities, something he never thought he had time for.

Ken had joined the dog obsessed. "Before Brando, everything was about me and my career. Then I got him and I thought, '*How can I make him famous?*' I forgot about advancing my own career and wanted to promote my dog."

Ken got his chance when he heard about the first Great American Mutt Show. On the day of the event, hundreds of people and dogs crowded a covered pier, and Brando didn't know what to think of it all. To bolster his confidence, Ken hoisted the dog into his arms, though he weighed about fifty pounds at the time. They watched several events before the one in which Brando was entered. As Brando watched, it was as if he thought, "*Oh, I go in the ring and run around. Okay. I can do that.*"

And he did, enjoying himself thoroughly and trotting off with second place in the Most Mixed Mutts category.

Following a move to Florida, Ken added a rottweiler mix and a pitbull to his and Brando's family. Dogs were becoming more and more a part of his life.

So the man who wasn't a dog person, the one who let a small mutt in Costa Rica change his life, wrote another book, *Dogs Who Found Me*. It was apparent: Ken Foster had gone to the dogs.

Turn about Is Fair Play

A frail old man shuffled into the Berrien County Animal Shelter in Nashville, Georgia. A knee-high brown dog bobbled along beside him on a leash.

"May I help you?" asked the woman behind the reception desk.

"Can you find my dog a good home?" the man said, his voice cracking with emotion. When questioned, he explained that his health required that he move in with his son, who was adamant that eight-year-old Sandy, a chow mix, could not accompany him.

His eyes brimmed with tears. "Please keep her safe," he begged Jeanette Genini, manager of the shelter at the time.

She looked down at the mutt, who smiled up at her. Sandy was definitely no beauty. "I promise," Jeanette said, knowing as she uttered the words that honoring the promise would be hard in a shelter that was always overcrowded.

But Jeanette managed, and six months later, Sandy was still safe at the shelter, a favorite of the staff who spent much of her time in the reception area. Even cats that roamed around the shelter seemed to love her.

The only ones who didn't love her were potential adopters. From time to time someone would ask about her, but when they learned that she was eight years old, they lost interest.

"Her looks didn't help either," Jeanette says. "Sandy is a designer dog that was apparently dreamed up by someone with a sense of humor." The dog smiled a lot, showing a mouthful of crooked teeth.

About that time, Hazel Blumberg-McKee of rural Tallahassee, Florida, logged onto Petfinder.com, looking for a dog. She had spent almost a year going from doctor to doctor, trying to figure out why she was so utterly exhausted all the time. Every part of her body ached. Finally, a rheumatologist diagnosed her ailment: fibromyalgia.

"The doctor said I needed at least thirty minutes of exercise every day," she says. Hazel had always walked, but now exercise sounded like a sentence rather than a pleasure. "I was so exhausted and in pain that it was hard to get motivated.

"Maybe I should get a dog as a walking buddy," she suggested to her husband, Jim. She knew as she said it that it would take a very special dog because the couple had sixteen rescue cats living in their home.

Hazel logged onto Petfinder.com and entered her search criteria. She needed an older dog that wasn't too full of boundless energy and, just as important, one who could tolerate animals of the feline persuasion.

When she saw Sandy's listing on Petfinder.com, a listing that proclaimed that the dog got along with cats, she called the shelter. "Her story broke my heart," Hazel explains, "so we went up on the weekend to see her."

Sandy was in her accustomed place in the reception area, and Hazel and Jim could hardly believe what they saw. "She was covered with cats," Hazel says. "Some were cuddling with her, others were chewing on her ears. She managed to shake them off and came over to say, 'Hi.'"

Hazel and Jim adopted Sandy and took her home, choosing the new name *Sadie* for their new dog.

Sadie nuzzled her way right into the family. "The cats forget she isn't a cat, until she barks, and then they go flying." Jim had not grown up around dogs, but he took to Sadie. "She has him totally twisted around her little dew claws and loves to manipulate him," Hazel says with a laugh. "She puts her head on his knee and looks pitiful until he notices. He goes to get the leash and off they go."

Hazel began her daily therapy walks, very short at first, with Sadie. Having always been an indoor dog, Sadie needed time to get used to this new adventure. Hazel was soon encouraged by their progress. "Now I just ask her if she wants to go for a walk, and she gets excited. She'll grab one of her stuffed toys and begin to squeak it and start running up and down the hall."

The regular exercise helped Hazel's fibromyalgia, and they lengthened their walks, exploring Hazel's and Jim's three acres of land and the surrounding woods.

Sadie had been on a glucosamine/chondroitin regimen for her aging joints as long as she had been with the family, but one day Hazel noticed that Sadie was stumbling during their walk. A visit to the veterinarian revealed that she had developed advanced osteoarthritis in her elbows. The vet started her on pain medication and suggested that, while walking was the best therapy for Sadie, they should cut the duration of their daily jaunts. The tables had turned, and Hazel was now Sadie's therapy person, taking her out for fifteen-minute walks several times a day. The regimen still met Hazel's need for at least thirty minutes of daily exercise.

The walking buddies took the changes in stride, remaining optimistic despite the challenges.

Neighborhood Watchdog

Lewis was sitting in one of his favorite spots, at the edge of his "mom and dad's" bed. From there, he had a fine view of the street and could keep his house safe from the aggressive cat that lived in the neighborhood and picked on kitties. After all, the thirteen-pound Chihuahua/dachshund mix had three cats of his own to protect.

Lewis's keen, chocolate-brown eyes surveyed the territory. No sign of the bully. But what was that coming down the street? He zeroed in on the unfamiliar sight.

In the other room, his "mom" was busying about with her household chores, leaving him to man (or dog, as it were) the second-story parapets, when she heard Lewis frantically barking. She knew his "bully cat" bark very well, but this was a different sound.

"I knew something was wrong," says Dejah Dorantes, who lives with her husband, Rick, the cats, and Lewis in Crockett, California. She hurried into the bedroom and looked out the window.

"There was a little toddler no more than eighteen months old, all alone, clutching a teddy bear, wandering down the hill toward a busy boulevard and freeway on-ramp."

She and the vigilant Lewis ran downstairs and outside.

"Lewis kept barking, wagging his tail, and jumping up and down to get the child's attention," Dejah says.

Fortunately, the sound of Lewis's barking carried down the hill to the little boy, and he stopped and turned. What he saw was a short-legged little tan-and-black dog, far more interesting to him than whatever lay at the bottom of the hill, so he began trudging back toward Lewis.

Lewis was still sounding the alarm. The child's mother heard the commotion and realized her baby had wandered out an open garage door. She raced out before Dejah made it to the street.

"After the rescue, I introduced the little boy to Lewis," Dejah says. "He got to pet our little hero. The tiny tot loved it as much as Lewis did."

Dejah rewarded Lewis with a medal and a gold star on his collar. The Dorantes were proud of their heroic dog, who had once been a throw-away.

"He and his four brothers were at the municipal shelter when Animal Rescue of Fresno found them," Dejah remembers.

Their friends had adopted Parker, one of Lewis's brothers, after seeing him on Petfinder.com, and they told the Dorantes about the Web site. When they saw what Dejah now calls her little "chi-boy," they decided to adopt him. It was the ideal match for Lewis because he could maintain contact with his brother.

"We get them together to play, and we all go camping together," Dejah says. "He loves riding in the boat."

Rick Dorantes is a volunteer firefighter, and Lewis soon became the unofficial mascot of Engine Company No. 79. He takes part in the September 11 commemoration each year at the fire station. He also participates in the Columbus Day Parade, riding in the fire truck with his "daddy."

When not involved in "official" duties, the thirteen-pound sentinel continues to staff his post on the bed, keeping a watchful eye on what is going on in the neighborhood.

Several months after the toddler rescue, Dejah again heard Lewis frantically barking and recognized that it was not the "bully cat" bark. She hurried into the bedroom to look out, and saw an unfamiliar husky dog headed down the hill toward the busy street. If he made it to the bottom of the hill, he would be in serious danger from the traffic.

Dejah and Lewis galloped downstairs and outside, with Lewis still sounding the alarm. Dejah managed to get the husky into the house, and while Lewis generously shared his chew toys with the dog, Dejah tracked down the owner, who had just moved in nearby. The husky, like the child, had escaped through an open garage door.

Lewis and the husky, who was named Demon, became friends, and one day Lewis raised the alarm again when he saw his pal trotting down the hill with two of his housemates. "Demon likes Lewis so much he came bounding for him, followed by his buddies, at a full run," Dejah says. "He bowled Lewis over, tail-over-tea-kettle. We then kept them busy romping playfully on the lawn until their owners, discovering the jailbreak, came out and retrieved them. One more date to inscribe on the hero medal he wears," Dejah boasts.

Without Lewis's vigilance, there's no telling what bad things would befall the neighborhood.

"What an alert, observant, and responsible neighborhood watchdog he has become," Dejah says. "Lewis has hero in his blood."

The Play's the Thing

As the saying goes, "Every dog has its day." Sam, a golden retriever, who belonged to the Del Rossi Family of Monroeville, New Jersey, was no exception. Michael, the eldest Del Rossi son, was playing Daddy Warbucks in a production of "Annie" at his school, and they needed a Sandy, the little orphan's canine ally. Michael volunteered Sam.

Sam took to stardom like a pro, according to his human mom, Christine. "He had a dressing room, and the students left treats for him each day. He seemed so disappointed when the play was over."

Sam passed away not too long after that, leaving the family with an elderly dog named Amber. With Sam gone, Amber seemed lonely, and the family began thinking about getting another pet to keep her company.

Matthew Del Rossi, then sixteen, logged onto Petfinder.com and zeroed in on a two-year-old named Blaze at Gloucester

County Animal Shelter. Matthew was sure he was the one. Christine, concerned about bringing a young dog into the family because of Amber's age, was unwilling to make any promises without meeting the dog. "Let me go see what he's like," she told Matthew.

Unfortunately, it was a holiday weekend and the shelter was closed. Matthew was afraid someone else would adopt the dog before he had a chance. To relieve his worry, Christine took off work Tuesday morning so she could be at the shelter when it opened.

Blaze was not a remarkable-looking dog. Creative license labeled him a German shepherd, but he only weighed forty pounds and his ears flopped over.

What Blaze did have going for him was his personality. He was a nice dog, and once the shelter staff reassured Christine about how Amber would relate to him, she was ready to adopt. "They said sometimes a younger dog peps the older dog up, and I do think Amber lived longer because she had Blaze's companionship. She tended to move around more."

Blaze had never lived in a house before. "The first time the television went on, he jumped and kept trying to find out what the noises were," Christine says. "But he adapted really well and now lives on the furniture and questions whether he wants to go outside for anything. He just lies around."

Once outside, however, his energy level shoots up. "We have a really big fenced yard with woods, and he races around so fast, it's like a blur," Christine explains. "I think he's part greyhound."

Not long after Blaze had settled in, the footlights beckoned, as they had with Sam. Michael Del Rossi, now out of high school, became the assistant director of a production of "Annie" at the local middle school. The director, remembering Sam's performance, asked if their family's dog could be in the play, not knowing that Sam had passed away. The director was surprised when Blaze showed up, but Christine assured him the dog would be fine.

Blaze had no formal obedience training, but he was so eager to please that he did quite well in his role. "Annie" also had a supply of treats so he would respond to her. Everything went well at rehearsals.

Then opening night arrived, and people filled the seats of the auditorium. The house lights dimmed, and the footlights came on. The show was about to begin.

"The first time the curtain opened," Christine recalls, "you could hear murmuring from the audience, like *'Oh how cute.'* There was just a lot of acknowledgment of a dog being on stage. He got scared and wanted to come to me."

"Annie" was belting out *Tomorrow*, and Blaze was dragging her toward the wings where he had spotted Christine, positioned there to manage him after his scenes. "Annie" gamely made it through the song, delivered Blaze to Christine, and on went the show.

First night jitters aside, Blaze did fine during the rest of the performances and took his much-deserved curtain calls with aplomb.

In place of a salary, Blaze got a free full-page ad in the program. Not forgetting his roots, he used the ad to put in a plug for Petfinder.com and Gloucester County Animal Shelter.

He retired from acting for the time being, but because Michael is the founder of the Broadway Bound Players, a drama program for young people, a comeback for Blaze is never out of the question.

A Smilin' Pit Bull

Melinda Gullo of Lakeview, New York, arrived home from work to find her boyfriend, Adam Davis, sitting in a roadside ditch, cradling an injured pit bull terrier. The dog had apparently been hit by a car and whimpered in pain every time Adam attempted to move.

The couple comforted the dog until the police and animal control arrived on the scene. The dog warden transported the dog to Orchard Park Veterinary Medical Center, a 24/7 emergency clinic in Orchard Park, New York.

"The dog won both of our hearts because he was so brave during the hour or so wait for a stretcher," Melinda says. Later the couple went door to door in the neighborhood, looking for his owner, but to no avail.

The accident had fractured the young dog's right foreleg, and he had suffered multiple abrasions on his head and legs. But his condition didn't suppress his sweet personality.

As Dr. Melissa Wajda splinted the dog's leg and gave him pain medication, she noticed what a sweetheart he was and couldn't help but worry about his fate. Animal Control, by law, would pay his expenses at the clinic, but if a stray wasn't claimed or adopted in five days, it would be euthanized. This dog's breed alone made the adoption from the town shelter unlikely because so many people fear pit bulls.

When the dog warden called to see how the dog was doing, Dr. Wajda asked if she could get in touch with a pit bull rescue group. The warden said that would be fine, and the vet knew just whom to call.

Eric Gray had recently moved to the area, and he operated Smilin' Pit Bull Rescue. Dr. Wajda had met him when he brought one of his dogs in for treatment a month or so earlier. The next day, Eric visited the clinic and took pictures of the dog Dr. Wajda named Eli. Time was ticking by, and still no one had claimed the dog. One of Eric's policies is that a dog must be neutered before it is adopted, so to make the dog more adoptable, the veterinarian donated her time to neuter Eli.

Meanwhile, Eric had posted information about Eli on his Petfinder.com Web site, hoping that someone would see the little fellow and want to give him a home. His photos showed a mostly black pit bull with a white chin and chest and a flash of white on his muzzle.

Several people inquired, and Eric went over their applications carefully.

"Pit bulls are very sweet dogs," he explains, "but because of their breeding they have a tendency for dog aggression. They don't have a trait for human aggression at all, as long as you socialize them properly. They make great family pets, but I think because of that aggression toward other dogs, they're best kept as only pets."

One application stood out. It belonged to Keri Stein, who lived just outside of Rochester, New York. She had no other pets and had pit bull and dog training experience.

"The first dog I ever had on my own was a pit mix," Keri says, "and she was the greatest dog I've ever had. Pit bulls are smart and loyal, and they're little comedians."

Keri had just bought a townhouse and wanted a dog, so she started looking at Petfinder.com. Many of the pit bulls in her area were listed by Smilin' Pit Bull Rescue, and she read about Eli.

"It said if no one took him, he would be put down in five days," she says. That was enough to convince her to contact Eric.

Eric told her the dog was a stray, so no one knew his background. Eric had, however, temperament tested him at the clinic and he seemed mellow.

"I didn't care what was wrong with the dog. I wanted him," Keri says. "If it turned out that he had dog aggression, we wouldn't go to the dog park. If he didn't like people, that is something you can train them out of."

On Eli's fifth day, no one had claimed him, so Eric called Keri. "How about a home visit?" he asked.

Keri agreed, and a little later Eric showed up with Eli, straight from the clinic.

Eli made a great first impression. He went right over to Keri, tail wagging. He checked out the house briefly, and then indicated, by standing by the door, that he needed to go outside for a pit stop.

"Can't beat that," Keri thought, *"he's already house trained."*

His broken leg didn't slow the one-year-old down. "He ran around on that leg as if the splint wasn't even there," Keri remembers. "We were trying to make him not do that—that was the biggest chore of all the month he had his cast on."

Keri renamed him Lennox, after Lennox Lewis, the British boxer. "I had about forty names picked out," she explains, "but since he might have some American Staffordshire in him, and the Staffordshire originated in England, and a pit bull is a fighting dog, I thought Lennox was appropriate."

Lennox's temperament test proved accurate, and Keri had a great new companion. "I can't understand why no one claimed him, because he's awesome," she says enthusiastically. "I take him to the dog park every other day, and he plays with all the dogs and swims in the water. He's very obedient and such a love bug. As long as he's in contact with you, he's the happiest dog in the world."

Lennox doesn't comment, of course, but his smile says it all.

A Sign of Love

When authorities raided this particular rural Missouri puppy mill, they seized over one hundred dogs. The "home sweet home" of the breeding females had been a semi-trailer, unheated in the winter and uncooled in the sweltering heat of Midwestern summers. Officers shut the place down and farmed the dogs out to various dog placement groups. Eighteen of them went to Second Chance Pet Adoptions, based in Smithville, Missouri.

Deanna Clark and other volunteers cleaned up the dogs entrusted to them and had a veterinarian check them for diseases, give them their shots, and neuter or spay them. Next, the placement group listed them on Petfinder.com and took them to adoption days to begin the task of finding permanent homes for the rescued pooches.

Among the dogs that Deanna tended was one cute little Maltese male who was about one year old. She named him *Lance*. Since Lance was not a breeding female, yet had not been sold, she surmised that the brokers who buy puppies from the millers had rejected him for some reason. He was such a cute little pup that Deanna figured his adoption would be immediate. Sure enough, before she'd had him a week, a woman applied to adopt him. Deanna was delighted. Now Lance would have a "forever" home.

A week later, Deanna was surprised when the adopter returned him, announcing that he was deaf.

"With so many dogs, it's hard to get to know each of them," Deanna says. "Lance involved himself in what the other dogs were doing, so I never noticed that he was hearing impaired. I understood, though, why the woman returned him. She was single and wanted a dog that would bark when someone came to the door."

Most shelters and placement groups have contracts in which adopters agree to return any pet they find unsatisfactory. Second Chance Pet Adoptions is no exception, and Deanna welcomed Lance back and re-entered his description and photo on Petfinder. com, this time with a special needs designation, noting that he was deaf.

Shelley Strelluf of Kansas City was looking for a dog to adopt to keep her company when her husband, Christopher, went off to basic training with the Army Reserve. She had allergies, so she had been checking out her reaction to various breeds her friends had.

"I didn't seem to have any trouble with Maltese, Shih Tzus, or Lhasas," explains Shelley, "but other dogs would make me sneeze and make my eyes water."

Shelley had spoken to several breeders about buying a dog, but she and Christopher knew there were thousands of dogs in shelters and placement groups, and they really wanted to help one out. She happened onto Petfinder.com and kept her eye on the site, looking for the perfect match.

"I was so excited when I saw Lance on the site," Shelley says, "but my heart sank when I saw the little special needs icon next to his picture. I wondered if he would need special accommodations that we wouldn't be able to offer or afford. When I read his description and found out he was deaf, I knew we could deal with that."

In fact, Shelley had a deaf dog when she was growing up, so it didn't seem like an insurmountable obstacle to her at all. "I called my husband and I called my mom. 'You have to see this dog,' I told them.'"

When she contacted the shelter, they told her their mobile adoption unit would be at a local shopping center the next day, and Lance would be there. Shelley knew she had to be there, too, so she called her boss and desperately pleaded to come in late on Saturday, and he agreed.

"Hey," she says wryly, "this was a family emergency."

She got to the shopping center parking lot right at 9:00 A.M., and the volunteers were still setting up. "A woman with three or four kids around her was holding Lance. She said they'd already adopted him."

Shelley was shocked. Close to tears, she sank down on a nearby curb.

A woman was sitting nearby. "You wanted that dog, didn't you?"

"Yeah, I really did," Shelley replied.

"That dog isn't right for those people," the woman said. "You go over there and get him."

Shelley looked toward the adoption table and saw that the people were handing Lance back to the volunteer.

"You'd better believe that I ran over, picked Lance up and haven't let go since," Shelley says.

The volunteer let Shelley take Lance to a little grassy area in the parking lot to get better acquainted. She sat with him for an hour. The little pooch was very frightened, and his posture reflected his fear. "But there was this little moment when his tail went up and he pranced," Shelley recalls, "and I thought, *'There's a dog in there with a lot of personality. He's just scared.'*" The other good news was that Shelley's allergies didn't act up while she was sitting with Lance.

The little dog that so appealed to her from the computer monitor was indeed the dog she wanted, and Shelley arranged to adopt him.

Going home, Lance crawled into her lap, but what appeared to be overwhelming trust at that moment didn't last. It took some time before he became the dog she saw a hint of when she first met him.

"He ran away when we came near him," Shelley remembers, "and the first month was pretty hard. But I spent a lot of time with him, and it was fun to watch him come out of his shell and start to play with his toys. Now he has so much confidence, he's a completely different dog. I don't think he knows he's small. He struts all over the place as if he's a big dog."

As far as Lance's deafness, the Strellufs have taught him signs for basic commands. They also discovered that he can hear high-pitched sounds.

The Strellufs live in an apartment, so Shelley takes Lance for walks three times a day, and he loves visits to the dog park. "He likes little dogs a lot. He doesn't hear the big dogs coming, so sometimes they run over him."

For Shelly, Lance was the answer to a prayer. "I've struggled with depression and, when my husband was gone, I would have my ups and downs. Some days I didn't even want to get out of bed. But then there was Lance, licking my face and reminding me that I had someone to keep me going. We saved each other."

Teacher's Pet

Max Gleeson is a fourth grader at St. Anthony Immaculate Conception school in San Francisco. He is rotten at spelling, and his math skills are zilch, but when it comes to deportment, Max leads the pack.

Each school day the seven-and-a-half-pound Yorkshire terrier trots into the classroom with his pet parent, Megan Gleeson, and assumes his place on her desk to wait for the kids to arrive.

Growing up, Megan always had a really big dog, so Max was quite a departure. But a big pooch simply wouldn't be comfortable in the apartment where she now lived. "I thought about getting a little dog, but I felt bad about the prospect of leaving it alone all day."

Meanwhile, Megan wanted a pet for her classroom, so she purchased a frog. "There really wasn't much interaction between it and the kids. You just had to drop a small pellet in a hole each day to feed it, and you couldn't pet it."

Then one day her principal suggested that Megan might want to get something a little more cuddly for her classroom.

"I rather jokingly asked, 'How about a dog?' and my principal was immediately open to it. She suggested I do some research, which I did, and I narrowed it down to a Yorkie."

Megan started looking for a purebred dog to buy, but they were all so expensive that they didn't fit into a teacher's budget. When she happened onto Petfinder.com and saw how many dogs needed homes, many of them purebreds, she knew that this was the answer to her problem. She would adopt a homeless dog. Among other things, doing so would set a good example for her students.

Max was a stray that Berkeley-based Small Breed Dogs Rescue had picked up in Oakland. "His photo on Petfinder.com was really cute," Megan says. "He's very photogenic, and he has humongous ears."

Megan worried that the little dog might be nippy, but the placement group assured her that Max wasn't, that he would get along with kids just fine.

The first night, Megan optimistically put Max in a crate in her bathroom. He began to cry, and the pitiful sounds wrenched her heart. "He was really, really stinky, so I took him out, gave him a bath, put a sweatshirt on a little footstool at the foot of the bed, and he spent the rest of the night there."

She hadn't told her students about Max. To get them ready, she had them write in their journals how they would feel about a classroom dog. "We had a lot of good discussion about it," she says.

Then the big day came: Max's first day of school.

"I left him in his crate in the classroom and they saw it and were talking about it. I explained how I had adopted him and about the responsibility of a dog in the classroom."

She laid down some ground rules and said that each day her two daily student assistants would make sure he had fresh water and food. "We tell time a lot in the fourth grade, so the assistants also would keep track of when he needed to go outside."

Another rule prohibited students from calling to Max during class. If he came up next to them, they could pet him, but they weren't to call him over.

Once Megan had gone over the rules, she had the students sit in a tight circle on the floor so Max couldn't get out. "I put him in the middle, and we threw a ball back and forth and let him come running. We talked about everything we knew about dogs for about half an hour."

Max fit in nicely. He especially liked to sit near the overhead projector, basking in the warm heat from its fan. Sometimes he spent his time in Megan's oversized office chair, snuggled between her and the back of the chair.

Megan noticed that Max sometimes trembled during school hours. "I always thought it was dumb to see dogs wearing sweaters, so I asked the vet about it. He told me to get a sweater and give it a try. So I did, and he stopped shaking. He didn't need it at home or when we went walking, but the school was a little chillier, and the sweater helped. When I would go and get his sweater and hold it up, he jumped up as if I were holding a treat."

Max soon had a wardrobe and the kids looked forward to seeing what the little clothes-dog would wear to school each day. Would it be the red turtleneck or his Harley-Davidson jacket that Megan's father bought for him? One Halloween he was a dinosaur; another year he was Toto to Megan's Dorothy. Of course, Megan carried him in a basket.

When Max needed surgery on his hind legs, the kids decided to hold a school-wide fundraiser. For one dollar, a child could have his or her photo taken with Max, who was sporting a sweater and hat.

"I think the best thing about having Max in the classroom is that it teaches the kids self-control," Megan explains. "It's challenging for nine- and ten-year-olds to not call him over. They also have to think about their actions and how they will affect Max. For instance, if they leave crayons on the floor, he eats them. If they push their chairs out without thinking, they may hit him accidentally because he's often underfoot. The children have to slow down and think."

Megan admits that he has taught her to be more responsible as well. "For instance, I have to get home in time to let him out. Of course, his excitement makes me feel good. He comes running to the door and is thrilled when I walk in."

Every morning at five o'clock, Max leaves his little bed and *tap, tap, taps* on the side of Megan's bed until she rouses. She lifts him up next to her for a little more slumber. Then, it is time to head for school where his classmates await him.

Mister Lucky

Keith Musgrove and thirty-five other firefighters from Hoover, Alabama, pulled into what had been a neighborhood of Waveland, Mississippi. Now it was a disaster zone. Hurricane Katrina had reduced the homes to rubble. The firefighters' task was to search every inch of that rubble for signs of life. As the men stepped out of their vehicles, they immediately saw one: a scruffy little dog. As the team walked over the debris—lumber, beams, plywood, trees, vehicles, furniture, roofs that were now on the ground—the little dog scrambled alongside them. He didn't want to be left behind again.

At nightfall, the men made their way to their tent camp a few blocks inland, and the dog followed. The little fellow looked liked Benji of movie fame, but the men started calling him *Lucky* for having survived the storm.

When the team returned to Hoover, Keith took Lucky with him and posted his description on the Petfinder.com Animal

Emergency Response Network (AERN) database. "I didn't put the location where we found him because I wanted to hold something back to help make a positive identification."

By the end of the week, Keith received fifteen to twenty e-mail responses. "Some were obviously not referring to this dog." But then he received one from Lee Ann Fial.

Lee Ann and Kenny Fial, their one-year-old daughter, Bevie Ann, and Lee Ann's mother decided to ride out Hurricane Katrina in their home rather than leave their nine dogs behind. They underestimated the fury of the storm.

As the hurricane intensified and the water began to rise, the family took all the dogs and retreated to the attic of their home. The house started disintegrating around them, and in the tumult, a rafter or a door—something—fell on Lee Ann's ankle and broke it. Two trees crashed down on the house, and the whole structure slipped from its foundation. The family struggled to the roof and huddled there with no assurance that they wouldn't soon be in the water because the house was now settling precariously. They spotted a small two-seated boat that had lodged in the debris and they crawled into it, pulling the dogs with them, to stay out of the water.

By that evening, they made it across the road to dry land and stayed there all Monday night.

Tuesday, the Coast Guard and people returning to check on their property found the Fials out on the street and evacuated the family. Lee Ann was airlifted to a hospital in Gulfport, while her mother and daughter, separately, went to a hospital in Bay St. Louis. Kenny, left behind, worried that no one was with Bevie

Ann, so he extricated a bicycle from the debris and pedaled to the hospital where she was taken. The dogs, on their own, scattered.

Lee Ann ended up at a special needs shelter where people were jam-packed eight to a room, and eventually had to return to the hospital to have her ankle put in a cast. Eight days passed before she found out where her family was.

"When I finally reached my mother, she burst out crying," Lee Ann recalls. They'd had no idea where Lee Ann was and if she was safe.

When the family established themselves in an apartment in West Point, Mississippi, Lee Ann got a computer and started looking for their dogs. She checked the AERN database every night. She also listed her missing pets in the "lost pets" section of the database.

As Keith Musgrove read Lee Ann's e-mail, it sounded as if Lucky was indeed her dog. The family had lived in the same neighborhood where Lucky had approached the firefighters, and to top it off, Lee Ann described the rainbow-colored collar Lucky was wearing.

"It was the craziest thing," says Lee Ann. "I put 'Looks like Benji' in my listing. When Keith listed him on the Web site, he put the same thing, 'Looks like Benji.'"

Keith and several of the other firefighters delivered Benji to his family, along with a trailer full of furniture, household supplies, and clothes collected by the Hoover Fire Department.

Keith was a little sad about giving up Lucky. The dog had been with him for six weeks, long enough to be firmly bonded. His kids had grown attached, and even his Labrador retriever accepted the little terrier.

"I never anticipated finding his owners," he says, his voice bittersweet. "When I brought him home, I thought I was bringing him home to keep." Nevertheless, Keith had done the right thing by giving a family who had lost so much a chance to reunite with a beloved family member.

Finding Carrie

From their place on the gravel bar, a mama dog and her puppies heard voices approaching. Around the bend in the river, a flotilla of canoes came into sight. The mama had once belonged to someone, so people weren't all that strange to her. Her pups, though, had never encountered humans. Frightened, they ran and hid.

The canoeists were part of a church group, led by their preacher. They pulled over on the gravel bar, which served as a take-out for boats. The mama dog, who was black and tan with a white chest and a hint of white on her long muzzle, approached them, ears alert. A few of her pups, following Mama's example, gathered their courage and ventured out of hiding.

When the church group reached civilization, the preacher reported the abandoned dogs to a woman who was involved in dog rescue. She, in turn, called another woman, Constance Fleming, who trekked down a dirt road to the access point for the river.

"The mama came right up to me," Constance says, "but it took a while to coax all the puppies out."

Constance took the dogs to Diana's Grove Dog Rescue, which Cynthia Jones founded at a 102-acre retreat for humans that she co-owned with Patricia Storm. Constance was a staff member at the retreat and served as an adoption caseworker for the dog rescue. While the canines awaited permanent homes, they ran free on the acreage and had dog-door access to all the buildings and the cabins where visitors stayed. The Grove was the epitome of dog friendly.

Constance named the mama dog *Carrie* and listed her and the puppies on Petfinder.com. Adopters snapped up the pups quickly, but Carrie was at the retreat for several months before Danique Rowsell of Novia Scotia spotted her on the Web.

Danique had been wanting a dog. She was in college and had left her pets behind with her family, but now she had found an apartment for the following fall that would allow pets.

"I grew up on a farm, around horses and going to horse shows," Danique relates. "People always had Australian shepherds or cattle dogs, and that's what I wanted." She also was interested in training a dog in agility.

Although she had set her heart on an Australian cattle dog, Danique soon concluded that she wouldn't have enough time to work such a dog, so she began to research other breeds.

"I looked at Jack Russell terriers but they had as much energy as a cattle dog except it came in a smaller package. I couldn't find breeders that I was happy with either. Too many were just in it for the money, not to improve the breed." At that point, Danique decided to adopt.

"One day I googled "Jack Russell terrier" and a rat terrier came up because it was identical to someone's Jack Russell," she explains. "So I began to look at information about rat terriers."

Danique contacted an animal welfare group in Ontario, and they put her name on a waiting list for a younger, but mature dog, twelve pounds or so, who could do agility competition. Meanwhile, they suggested she look on Petfinder.com, where they list their pets.

Danique began looking at rat terriers all over the states. Eventually her search led to Missouri.

"At the bottom of one of the last screens showing me all the rat terriers in Missouri was this dog that just made me stop," she recalls. "She was perfect. A rat terrier/Australian cattle dog mix, two years old and in need of an active home. It even stated what a wonderful agility prospect she'd be." It was Carrie.

Danique wrote a long e-mail, saying how gorgeous Carrie was. Several hours later she had a response from Constance. They e-mailed back and forth and then spoke on the phone before Constance was certain that Danique was a good match for Carrie.

The adoption was approved, but the next hurdle was getting Carrie to Nova Scotia. Danique was in school, but fortunately her mother agreed to fly to Missouri to pick up the dog.

When Carrie arrived at the Rowsell's home in Nova Scotia, Danique began to question what she had done. "I had to coax her out of her kennel. She was timid and shaking and wouldn't go near anyone but my mom. She didn't get along with the other dogs that well. I had told my seven-year-old sister, Natacha, that she had to take care of Carrie while I went back to school to finish the semester, and she was excited. Then Carrie nipped at her. Natacha was heartbroken. I went from a high to the lowest low."

But a transformation came quickly. After a week and a half, Carrie had adjusted to her new surroundings.

"She snuggled and played and kissed everyone she met," Danique says. "She responded to being called, and she got along with the cats and horses. Most of all, she loved being loved more than anything in the world. Her eyes lit up with *thank yous* every time we petted her. Her tail wagged, full of love, every time someone said her name."

Danique's seventeen-year-old sister, Alexandra, hadn't paid much attention to Carrie. She had her own interests, mainly horses. Then she suffered a head injury while riding and lost her short-term memory. After the accident, the dog surprised everyone by focusing on Alexandra. Carrie began to follow her from room to room. She slept with her and sat by her at the table. She gave Alexandra her undivided attention as she recovered.

Carrie had already become the kind of companion Danique had envisioned, but her special sensitivity around Alexandra showed that she had more of the right stuff than anyone had imagined. It was enough for Danique to enroll her in Canine Good Citizen training in hopes of using her as a therapy dog. The little foundling had found her calling.

Everybody Needs a Buddy

When Matt and Maria Hixson of Lubbock, Texas, wanted to adopt a dog as a companion for their children, Adam and Amanda, they weren't sure what kind would be best. Matt located an online breed selector, typed in answers to the questions it posed, and clicked *Enter*. Although Matt is a firefighter, he was surprised when Dalmatian, a breed long associated with firefighters, popped up as an appropriate choice for the Hixsons' lifestyle.

Matt logged onto Petfinder.com and searched for Dalmatians. One named Buddy was listed by Leland's Heart Sanctuary in the nearby town of Hurlwood, Texas.

Leann Landmesser, who ran the Sanctuary, told Matt and Maria that Buddy came to her after his owner relinquished him to a veterinary clinic. He had been with Leann for about a year, but she had recently joined Petfinder.com and posted his photo and description on the site. Buddy was soon to become her first Petfinder adoption.

Buddy impressed the Hixsons, and when Leann brought Buddy to their house for her required home visit, the dog was just as impressed. "He walked in and seemed to say, 'I'm home,'" Leann recalls happily.

The Hixsons adopted the three-year-old on Christmas Eve.

"My wife suggested that I take Buddy to the station and introduce him to everyone and see how this 'fire dog' handled himself," says Matt. "The first shift was a little difficult. We have the only two-story fire station in town, and Buddy had never seen stairs before."

Matt began to train Buddy to go on fire runs. He would sit in the cab of the fire engine while the crew battled a fire.

Then late one cold night, the alarm sounded. The firefighters jumped into their gear and headed to the truck. Buddy was reluctant to jump in the cab, so Matt tried to lift him in, but it was obvious the dog didn't want to go. Seconds ticked by. There was no time to coax him, so Matt told him to stay. Matt himself jumped on the truck and away it sped.

"I had the rank of firefighter at that time, and I rode on the back," Matt says. "I looked back at the fire station as we drove away. The door was coming down, and I saw Buddy slip out under the door."

He was horrified. The perfect dog was going to get lost, and there was nothing he could do about it. It was cold and dark and beginning to snow.

The emergency turned out to be a broken water line in a commercial building, and the firefighters were able to return to the station forty-five minutes later. Matt's fear was realized: Buddy was gone.

The crew fanned out and searched the area. After a while, they returned to the station, empty-handed.

As Matt dejectedly started up the back stairs, he spotted Buddy underneath the stairwell. "He had apparently crawled under the fence and had come in the back door, which was propped open. Then he crawled under the stairs and waited for us."

Matt was incredibly relieved. But the experience ended Buddy's fire runs, although he still accompanied Matt to graduations at the training academy and to schools during Fire Prevention Week.

"Anywhere I take him, people flock to him," Matt says proudly.

"As a firefighter, I'm gone for twenty-four hours, and then home for forty-eight," Matt explains. "It's great to be greeted by Buddy. He's always glad I'm home, and his great big smile really brightens my day."

Everybody needs a Buddy. The Hixsons found one.

Going to Kansas City

The white chow chow was like a ghost that manifested from time to time in Debbie Dodd's neighborhood in Huntsville, Alabama. No one knew where he had come from and Debbie, concerned for him, began to put food out. After about a year, his appearance began to decline, and Debbie decided it was time for more serious human intervention. When her attempt to get near the chow chow failed, Debbie resorted to a humane trap, and late one night, a neighbor called to say the dog had been captured.

"As I approached, I wasn't sure what I was in for," Debbie says. She became even more wary as the dog let out a deep warning growl. But even that wasn't going to stop her. This dog needed human help, and she was just the person to give it—she ran an animal welfare organization called A New Leash on Life.

Debbie opened the cage, speaking gently to the dog, and extended her hand. He appeared terrified, but somehow Debbie managed to get him out and into her truck.

"He never growled at me again, and he never tried to bite me," she recalls. He seemed to know that Debbie was a guardian angel who had come to help him.

Once home, she shaved off the hard mats of fur that covered him, finding, in the process, an embedded rusty choke collar. It made her suspect he had broken loose from being chained in someone's backyard and had fled, never to return. She got him cleaned up and took him to the vet, who vaccinated, dewormed, and neutered him.

Debbie's mom solved the question of what to name the pooch. She suggested Klondike, and it seemed to fit the dog, who, when cleaned up, was as white as Klondike snow.

Knowing how long he had been on his own, Debbie was not in a hurry to tame him. She let him loose in her backyard to warm up to his new life gradually.

"He slowly became used to the feeding routine and to me," Debbie explains, "but he was unsure of everything else. If anyone came over to visit, he would run and hide under our pool house with his best friend, Blondie," another rescued dog.

From Blondie, Klondike learned to use the doggy door, although it took him four months to try it, even with her example, and he remained wary of approaching people.

"The major breakthrough came at six months," recalls Debbie. "One night when I was sitting alone at the kitchen table, reading my mail, Klondike slowly walked up to me and licked my hand. He had never approached me before. I always had to go to him—and very slowly."

It took longer for Klondike to trust other people. "I would put him on a leash when people came over and I made him sit with me while the 'stranger' approached him. He would tremble all over while the person petted him."

Debbie never intended to keep Klondike permanently because rescuing homeless pets and finding "forever" homes is what she does. So at a certain point in Klondike's social rehabilitation, she posted his photo and description on Petfinder.com.

Across the country in Kansas City, Missouri, Margaret Monteleone was browsing on the Internet when she happened onto the Petfinder.com Web site. The Monteleones' chow chow Kato had passed away a year earlier. They also had an old chow named Miko, but Kato's death definitely left a gap in the family. To fill it, they adopted Smokey, a chow/keeshond mix, from Wayside Waifs in Kansas City, but though he was a great dog, he didn't click with them the way Kato had.

"Klondike's picture on Petfinder just reached out and grabbed me," Margaret says. "He looked so much like Kato. I printed out his picture and showed my husband. This man has never been on a vacation in his life, so I thought there was no way he was going to take off and drive to Alabama to adopt a dog—but I just wanted him to see the picture."

Nick Monteleone's response surprised her. "He's gorgeous. I really want that dog."

They called Debbie, and after she screened their adoption application, she agreed that they would be a good match for Klondike, so the Monteleones made plans to head south.

Debbie wanted them to stay two nights so Klondike would have a longer time to get acquainted before he set off for his new home.

"I told her that we couldn't be gone that long because of our other dogs—Miko is twelve and very decrepit," Margaret says. "Debbie insisted we bring them along and that we stay at her house. She gave us the whole upstairs. She was just so gracious."

Because it was late when they arrived, the Monteleones only got a quick look at Klondike in the backyard that first night. The next morning, they went outside to begin getting acquainted.

"Whenever we'd go near him," Margaret recalls, "he'd get the fenced pool between us and him." She had to keep an eye on Smokey, a reformed fence jumper. At home, they'd installed an electric wire along the top of their fence. The pooch had tried it once, and that was the end of his escapades there. But in Alabama, it was a whole new ballgame. The six-foot fence was merely a challenge. That left Nick to woo Klondike into trusting him.

"Nick was putting in a lot of time getting acquainted. Klondike was fine once you were near him, but approaching him just wasn't going to happen," Margaret explains.

Sunday came, and it was time for the Monteleones to leave. Debbie was despondent. She and her husband had cared for Klondike for ten months. Letting him go was so hard. So hard, Margaret almost backed out of taking him from Debbie. But Debbie knew these people were perfect for Klondike, so she stiffened her resolve and watched them drive away.

"I felt I was betraying him," Debbie says sadly. "I cried for a week." But she knew he was in a good place, and the Monteleones kept in touch, telling her of Klondike's progress.

Once in his new home, Klondike and Smokey, both still young dogs, became best buddies. They romped and played in the backyard like two little kids.

Klondike was still reluctant to approach people. "When I go out to bring him in at night, he won't come right over to me," Margaret explains. "If I get down and make a fuss over one of the other dogs, then Klondike will come up behind me. It's like one step forward and two back."

A step forward came one day when Margaret saw him at the sliding glass door. "Usually if I walk toward the door, he runs off the deck. But I opened the door and he came in. I ran into the other room and told Nick that Klondike had come in on his own.

It was so exciting. It was like seeing a little kid learn to walk and talk, and you look at each other and say, 'Isn't that cute?' We wonder what could have possibly happened to make him so afraid of people. For us, this wonderful animal has helped heal the pain of losing Kato. We just hope that whatever happened to him starts to dull in his memory as well."

Many Hands, Many Hearts

Melinda Henke-Sauer and Melissa Hane tied a pink bandana around the old dog's neck and attached a poem they had written about her to her kennel. The two women were board members of the Association for the Protection of Animals (APA) in Granite City, Illinois, and were at Lambert International Airport in St. Louis, saying their tearful goodbyes to a Hurricane Katrina evacuee named Nikki. She was on her way to Dallas and from there to Shreveport, where her eighty-three-year-old owner, Odette Koeller, awaited her.

The ten-year-old chow/Labrador retriever mix had been on quite an adventure since the day the hurricane blew into New Orleans and disrupted her family's life.

"We had a two-story house," Odette recalls, "and we didn't think it was going to be as bad as it was. We had to run from Hurricane Ivan a year earlier, but it didn't damage the house. We thought it would be the same with this one. My daughter and I left on August twenty-seventh, and I only took a couple of dresses and some old shoes because we thought we'd be back in a couple of days. Wrong!"

Her daughter, Janice Cosey, son-in-law, John, and Odette went to Houston, leaving Nikki with Odette's daughter-in-law, Sherron McCoy and her son and daughter, Reginald Koeller III and Anjelle Koeller. When predictions about the storm worsened, Reginald, a New Orleans police officer, took his mother and sister to the Superdome, where the rules did not allow pets. They had left a supply of food and water on the second floor of the house for Nikki and prayed for the best. When Reginald eventually was able to get back to the house, a painted message on the door indicated that rescuers had found one animal alive and had evacuated it. The date suggested the dog had been alone for twenty days.

Odette Koeller sighed with relief when she heard the news, but she missed her dog terribly. Nikki had been her solace after the death of her husband a year earlier. She desperately wanted to find her but had no idea where to begin looking.

Odette and her family relocated to a farm near Shreveport that belonged to a distant cousin. As soon as Janice could get to a library with public access computers, she put information about Nikki on the Animal Emergency Response Network (AERN) database set up by Petfinder.com when Hurricane Katrina struck.

"I was so afraid Nikki might be put to sleep when she was found because of her age

In her message she directed anyone with information to contact her brother, Reginald Jr., who had relocated to Dallas after the hurricane. "He already had a computer set up," Janice explains.

Meanwhile she also contacted Adoption Pet Services, an animal welfare group in the greater New Orleans area, asking for help locating the dog. Arvella Lesnak responded by forwarding the request to other animal welfare folks across the country.

After reading the request, Janet Corbett of the Wildwood Pet Network in Fairfield, Ohio, began searching "found pet" reports on the AERN Web site, looking for a dog that matched Nikki's description. She only knew that Nikki was a honey-colored Lab/chow mix and had been shaved recently. Out of thousands of possibilities, she narrowed it to four photos and sent them to Janice Koeller. One of them was a photo of a dog being given a bath at the APA.

A representative from the shelter had gone to New Orleans after Katrina and had transported nine dogs back to Illinois. Their photos were posted on AERN. One of them was Nikki.

Almost simultaneously someone who knew Anjelle Koeller saw the notice Janice had posted and contacted Reginald Jr. in Dallas and said she thought she had seen their dog on Petfinder. com. He, in turn, e-mailed APA.

In Illinois, Melissa Hane opened Reginald's e-mail message. It said he thought Goldie, the name APA had given Nikki, was his mother's dog. Correspondence and photos flew back and forth until all of them were certain: This was a match. Everyone was jubilant.

Plans for a reunion were made, and Melinda and Melissa drove Nikki to the airport and said goodbye. When Reginald Jr. reached the cargo area at Dallas-Fort Worth International Airport, Nikki was waiting in a large crate. "When I walked in the door, her back was to me. I said, 'Is that the Nikki pup pup?'"

It was the familiar way he had greeted her when the family was all at home in New Orleans. She knew that voice. The crate began to shake as she stood up and began to paw its door. She whimpered, and her tail began to wag. Reginald took her out, and she leaped for joy. This was family.

He took her for a walk, then she rode shotgun all the way to Shreveport. He could have sent her by plane, of course, but he didn't want to miss the look on his mother's face.

Two months to the day after Katrina ravaged the coast, Reginald Jr. delivered Nikki to his mother in a smothering of kisses and hugs.

The Journey Home

Angels were watching over me
And took me far away.
There I stayed for eight long weeks,
But I'm going home today.
They treated me with love and care
And loved me as their own.
A dry warm place to lay my head,
A frequent pat and bone.
Today is the day I bid goodbye
And thank them for their love.
Home is where I'm flying now,
Flying on a big white dove.

—BY MELINDA HENKE-SAUER AND MELISSA HANE

The House That Jake Built

The one-eyed mini-American Eskimo dog was making rounds at the hospital walking track when Deena Hallman's mother spotted him. She called her daughter, who is director of Newberry County Animal Care and Control in Newberry, South Carolina.

Deena was pretty sure who the dog was. She had picked up the little escape artist before. Her colleague at the shelter, Tina Bishop, knew him, too. She referred to him as "a little Houdini."

By the time Deena got to the hospital track, Jake had gone on to greener pastures, but that evening, Deena got a call from a video store in Newberry. "Jake had apparently gone in to rent a movie," Deena says wryly, "and the lady at the store didn't think it was such a good idea." Deena hurried over, and this time she nabbed the little fellow.

"I think this was the third time I'd picked him up," she recalls. His owner's yard had a picket fence they had put up for him, and there weren't any holes in it. "From what we could figure, he was hitting the top of the air conditioner and springing off of it to get out."

After one of his escapes, the owners didn't return Deena's calls, so she drove out to Jake's house. "They said they just couldn't keep him in anymore, so they signed him over to us, which meant we could put him up for adoption immediately."

The shelter posted him on its Petfinder.com pet list and waited, but no one e-mailed or called about a partially blind Eskie who had a reputation for escape.

Meanwhile, the staff at the shelter grew to love the dog, who was about four years old. "He was so sweet," Tina says. "He loved taking rides in the truck with us. We took him along when we went to pick up lunch."

A month passed before Deena looked at her e-mail and found an inquiry from Robert Blankenship. Robert had moved into his mother's house in Richlands, Virginia, after ending a long-term relationship. Among other things he lost in the break-up were his partner's two American Eskimo dogs he'd learned to love, *learned* being the operative word. At first, one of them had threatened to bite him every time he moved.

"When I came out of the bathroom," Robert remembers, "teeth and fur just came flying at me." But the pooch came around and became very loving. Both dogs won Robert's affection, and he became an Eskie lover, which led him to a Yahoo! group called just that—Eskie Lovers.

Robert wanted his own Eskie, so he went on Petfinder.com to find one. The moment he read Jake's description, he figured he needed to adopt the little escape artist because the dog didn't have much going for him.

When Robert's application was approved, he shared the good news on Eskie Lovers.

Sarah Hale, a Tennessean who also posted on the site, congratulated him and asked if he wanted some help getting Jake.

Robert e-mailed Sarah and invited her to go along, providing she would cook breakfast for him when he got to her house. She replied that she would cook, but only if he would wash the dishes.

Robert left in the middle of the night and swung over to Tennessee. He and Sarah had been e-mailing back and forth, but this was the first time they had met in person. Now, they set out to get Jake.

"Robert was at the shelter when we opened the gate at ten o'clock," Deena Hallman recalls. She was delighted that someone wanted the little dog.

When Robert and Sarah arrived back in Tennessee, Jake met his new friend's two mini-Eskies, Lily and Kobi, and they all got along fine.

"Jake and I got snowed in at Sarah's, in a massive, almost quarter-inch snow," Robert jokes, "and we never left."

Robert discovered that Jake's reputation as an escape artist was not overblown. "The yard is fenced, but Jake got out three times in an hour, and I had to patch the fence. It looks like a patchwork quilt now."

As for Jake's blind eye, which Deena Hallman speculated was probably from an injury, it didn't slow him down a bit. "He runs like a maniac," Robert boasts. "At one place he jumped our fence at forty-eight inches, and he's only twelve inches tall. He just takes off running and jumps."

After Jake brought Robert and Sarah together, all that was left was to make it permanent. The couple married in September 2005.

Now it was one big happy household—the house that Jake built.

A Labradoodle To-Do

The female black poodle was quite a beauty and had American Kennel Club papers to show why. Of course her lineage didn't matter to the Labrador retriever next door, but he thought she was rather fetching.

The result of his attraction was Frosty, a white labradoodle, who was considered an unfortunate mistake by the poodle's owner. So when Frosty was four months old, her mistress crated the pup and relinquished her to Red River Society for the Prevention of Cruelty to Animals in Gainesville, Texas.

Frosty showed her enthusiastic demeanor as she bounded out of the crate at the shelter. She ran right into the arms of Tommie Kirksmith, the shelter manager, as if she'd known the woman forever.

"Frosty jumped up—her paws nearly reached my waist—and lavished kisses on my hands and arms," remembers Tommie, who instantly loved the dog.

The labradoodle, with her wonderful temperament, was a model citizen among her sheltermates. Whenever Tommie had to even out the count between the "rowdy dog" yard, the puppy yard, and the backyard, she would move Frosty because she could rest assured that the easygoing dog would fit in anywhere.

"Each time I did this, whichever yard Frosty occupied became the 'yard of the week,' behavior-wise," Tommie says.

It was fortunate for Tommie that Frosty was a good dog because no one was in any hurry to adopt her. Visitors came and went, found dogs they liked, adopted them, and took them to new homes. But no one chose Frosty. In spite of the fact that in some parts of the country people actively sought labradoodles to train as service dogs, the people who visited Red River SPCA regarded her as something of a joke. One person called her the "Lab with the bad hair day."

After Frosty had been at the shelter for several months, Tommie signed her organization up with Petfinder.com and began to post pet descriptions and photos on the site. Frosty was the twelfth dog she listed on Petfinder.

Five days later she received an e-mail from Valerie Roulo. "My family and I are in the process of looking to adopt a dog," it read. "Growing up, we had a poodle for sixteen years, and we recently lost a beautiful yellow lab we'd had for twelve years to bone cancer. When I came across Frosty, I thought she was just wonderful. Could you please tell me more about her?"

Tommie was thrilled. Here was someone who had owned a poodle and then a Lab. Frosty sounded perfect for the Roulos.

She invited them to come and meet her. What Valerie left out of her e-mail is that they lived across the country in New Hampshire.

The distance had postponed Valerie's initial inquiry. "When I saw that Frosty was in Texas, I thought that was the end of the idea. My family had decided that we would look for a dog we could drive and get—a couple of states away, tops—not clear to Texas. So I went to bed that night sad at how far away Frosty was."

At 3:00 A.M., unable to sleep, she got out of bed and went to the computer. Valerie, a widow, and her daughter, Emily, lived in an apartment in her parents' home. Both she and her folks have their own computers, so Valerie e-mailed Frosty's photo to her parents. "This is the dog I want; she is perfect," she typed.

The next morning her mother urged her to find out more about Frosty, so that was when Valerie first e-mailed Red River SPCA. She was surprised when Tommie replied within an hour or so. In subsequent e-mails Valerie explained that she was in New Hampshire, but learned that Tommie would consider an out-of-state adoption.

For the next three weeks, the two women talked on the phone and e-mailed back and forth. Tommie sent new photos of Frosty and ascertained that the Roulos would be a good placement for Frosty. The Roulos arranged to have Frosty flown from Texas to New Hampshire.

"We sent the adoption fee and a donation to the shelter for all the kindness and work Tommie did to make the adoption happen," Valerie says. "She went above and beyond because she wanted the five-hour trip to be the least traumatic for Frosty. She practiced getting Frosty into the kennel she would be traveling in. Every night, Tommie would report in to tell us how Frosty did."

The big day finally arrived. Tommie crated Frosty and took off for Dallas/Fort Worth International Airport. She drove through a labyrinth of buildings to find the Priority Parcel station, completed the necessary paperwork, and then took Frosty on a leash to a grassy area for a last pit stop before the flight. Tommie was glad Frosty was going to a new home, but was in no hurry to put her on the plane. She had grown quite fond of this endearing young dog.

A fine mist of autumn rain was falling, and as it got heavier, Tommie knew it was time to take Frosty in and say their goodbyes.

While Tommie was feeling reluctance, across the country, the Roulos were feeling anticipation. They drove to Boston to pick up Frosty.

"As we were getting ready to leave, my phone rang and it was Tommie, just letting us know that Frosty was on her way," Valerie recalls. "I will never forget the sound of her voice. She was very happy that Frosty was coming to New Hampshire, but it was hard for her, too."

The Roulos arrived at the airport about two hours ahead of time. They located the area where Frosty would be arriving and settled in to wait. Time passed sluggishly.

At last, a luggage cart appeared and two men hoisted a kennel from it onto a conveyor belt. Slowly it came their way. Valerie, her daughter, and her mom all exclaimed, "Frosty!"

Frosty herself wore a big smile, gazing through the bars of her crate. Her tail thumped against the sides.

"I opened the cage," recalls Valerie, "and was greeted with the biggest hug. She was so excited that you could tell she was thinking, 'You must by my new family that Tommie told me about; now where is that little girl?' She stopped hugging me and ran to my daughter and gave her a hug."

A crowd had gathered, watching what appeared to be a family reunion, tears and all.

"As we were all walking out of the airport," says Valerie, "I heard a woman comment, 'Boy! They're glad to have their dog home.'"

Frosty's new "forever" family beamed. It was true. Frosty was their dog, and she was home where she belonged at last.

Sentimental Journeys

When Rob Pisani of Arlington, Virginia, saw a photo of Coco on Petfinder.com, his jaw dropped. The dog was the spitting image of his beloved Sammy, a seven-year-old miniature poodle who had recently passed away after a short battle with skin cancer. Not only had Rob been despondent over the loss of his dog, but Dave, his other seven-year-old miniature poodle, missed Sam as well. The dogs had been together since they were pups.

"At first I thought the resemblance to Sam was just a bit too spooky, so I didn't contact the foster group which had listed Coco," Rob says.

When he changed his mind and e-mailed Debby Speroni at Community Animal Rescue & Education (C.A.R.E.) in Carterville, Illinois, Rob was too late. Someone else had already spoken for Coco. A few days later, however, Rob received an e-mail saying the other person had backed out and Coco was his, if he would come and get her.

That seemed problematic to Rob. After all, he lived nine hundred miles from Carterville, and he was an attorney with a hectic schedule. He simply didn't have time to make the trip, and he didn't believe in shipping a dog as cargo.

Destiny had a different idea.

"I was called to a business meeting in Columbus, Ohio. I could fly from Columbus to Illinois, pick up Coco and fly home." The change in the flight plan would cost him an extra two hundred dollars, he learned, but Rob figured the dog was worth it.

Things went from good to better. "When I got to the airport in Columbus to change my ticket, I told the woman at the counter I was going to Illinois to adopt a poodle," Rob says. "When she heard that, she 'comped' the difference in fare."

At an airport in Evansville, Indiana, Rob rented a car and headed to Carterville, where he checked into a motel. "I told the woman at the motel about Coco, and she said, 'Oh, you're going to Debby's. I won't charge you for the night.'"

Feeling as if this adoption was meant to be, he finally met Coco the next morning. "He jumped right into my lap," Rob recalls, "and he looked so much like Sam, even down to the racing stripe along his back." Coco was technically an apricot poodle but, in fact, was almost white.

The adoption finalized, Rob headed to Nashville where he could get a direct flight home. About midway, the airline called him on his cell phone and said the flight had been cancelled. "I thought, 'Now what do we do?' Coco was sitting in my lap and just then he put both paws on the wheel as if to say, 'We'll drive.' So we did."

Coco was a good traveler and spent most of the trip in Rob's lap, just as Sam had done on car trips. Thirteen hours later they arrived home. Now came the real test: meeting Dave.

When they entered the hall at Rob's condo, he took Coco off-leash. "He didn't hesitate; he knew right where to go," says Rob. "He passed several units and went right to the door of my apartment. He sat there waiting for me to catch up. Now I'm thinking that this is all too strange—as if Coco had Sammy's spirit tagging along."

Rob opened the door and Dave came running out. "He took one look at Coco and then did a doggy double-take. I'm sure at first he thought Sam was back. Then he started trying to get Coco to play. There was no snarling, no biting. Within an hour, they were snuggled up together on the bed with me. It was as if this had been Coco's home for a long time."

Rob stayed in contact with C.A.R.E., and on one cross-country trip, took Coco back to visit Debby Speroni. He also called Coco's former owner, who had given the dog up when she had to move to an assisted-living facility in California to be near a family member. Rob assured her that Coco was in a happy home.

Several years after Coco's adoption, Rob's father passed away, and his mother, who lived in Florida, was lonely. "She knew my dogs and said she might like to have a dog, too. I asked her what kind, and she said a poodle would be good."

Once again Rob logged onto Petfinder.com and entered his search criteria. Back came a list that matched his query. The poodle at the top of the list was named Joey. A chill went up Rob's spine. His dad's name was Joe. Not only that, but the poodle was at C.A.R.E. in Carterville.

Rob felt that Sam's spirit had led him to Carterville once, now it seemed as if his dad's spirit was guiding him back to Illinois on a second rescue journey.

Traveling Life's Roads

Barkley McCarthy rides a Harley. He doesn't operate the clutch or the gears. Instead the little dog—probably a cockapoo—nestles inside a pack against the chest of his "mom." His head pokes out, and he gazes down the road through his 'Doggles,' watching the bike eat up the miles. Life hasn't always been so carefree for Barkley or his owner, Carol McCarthy of Bound Brook, New Jersey.

Several years earlier, Carol's fox terrier had developed bladder cancer, and she tended him through fourteen months of illness before he died. Once over her grief, she began to look for another dog on Petfinder.com. She wanted an adult pooch because, besides a full-time job, she had a one-hour commute on either side of her workday. A puppy couldn't tolerate being alone that long.

Barkley met her criteria. He was four or five years old when Animal Rescue Force (ARF), a New Jersey animal welfare organization, pulled him from a Staten Island shelter. He spent his weeks with a foster family and weekends in a kennel at one of the two permanent flea market booths the group had run for years.

Carol had seen two ARF dogs on Petfinder.com that she was interested in, so on the weekend she went to the flea market where ARF planned to have the first of the dogs. As it turned out, he was sick, so volunteers hadn't brought him out. They told her the other dog was at their second location in Englishtown, New Jersey, and Carol decided to trek down to see him. She found the ARF booth, and there in the third tier of stacked cages sat the second little guy she'd seen on the Web site.

"He was so scared," Carol says. "When I picked him up, he literally wrapped his front legs around my neck and wouldn't let me go."

Once in his new home, the dog proved to be very well behaved. To Carol's delight, he never chewed anything and was already housebroken. He seemed to have been trained, although he didn't respond to the commands Carol gave him.

Four days later Carol found out why. The animal welfare group forwarded a paper to her that they had received from the shelter. It revealed that the dog's original name was Pepo and that he only understood Spanish.

Carol put the paper down, looked at the little pooch and commanded, "Siéntese," and the dog, by then named Barkley, sat, as Carol had instructed—in Spanish. In no time at all, Carol joked, he passed English as a Second Language, and Barkley had found a great "mom" and a best friend in Carol.

Six months after Carol discovered Barkley's bilingual abilities, their lives catapulted into chaos when she learned she had cancer. The doctors scheduled her for major surgery, and her mother and brother came down from Buffalo to be with her and to stay with Barkley while Carol was in the hospital.

"When I came home from the hospital, I was absolutely wasted," says Carol. "Everybody was concerned about Barkley jumping on me because of the surgery. I said, 'Just let him come in.'"

Carol had settled herself into an extra-wide chair and she had pillows around her to protect her long incision. Barkley jumped up beside her and laid his head on her chest. "Normally he would jump all over me, but he knew." He had missed her so much, and she had missed him.

When Carol underwent chemotherapy, Barkley was her devout companion. She was able to work from home during the treatment period, and he most often sat on her lap as she worked at the computer. He didn't want her out of his sight.

"When I was tired, I would go to the couch to rest, and he would go with me," Carol recalls. "Sometimes he would literally come and lie on my chest as if to say, 'I'm not going to let you up. You need to rest.' It was a comforting thing. I called him Dr. Barkley, and I would tell him I was going to be there for him—that he didn't need to worry."

When Barkley's first anniversary with Carol rolled around, she had almost finished her chemotherapy. She was between treatments and feeling good, so she threw a Coming Home Day anniversary party for him. Her family came from Buffalo, bringing with them special dog treats. The festivities included a cat-shaped piñata filled with dog goodies. Carol made party hats and hors d'oeuvres fit for a dog, and she asked the human guests to shower Barkley with gifts that he could donate to a local animal shelter. Barkley did get one gift to keep: his Doggles—goggles for motorcycle-riding dogs.

The following day, Carol adjusted Barkley's Doggles, snuggled him into the pack that fit across her chest, climbed aboard her Harley Road King for the first time since she had gotten sick, and they took a ride—his first. He loved it.

Barkley and Carol were a perfect match. "I found him when he needed me most, and he was there when I needed him most, when I discovered I had cancer."

Two years after Carol's surgery, the pair added a "dad" to their family. "Frank had never had a dog," Carol says, "but he dotes on Barkley the way I do." The McCarthys are now traveling life's roads together.

Full House

The description of the Australian cattle dog at Perry County Humane Society recounted a bleak story. The pup had been living in the wild for quite some time before animal control in Pinckneyville, Illinois, was able to capture him. The Humane Society took the starving dog in, and their kennel became his home for five months. They listed him on Petfinder.com and even ran his photo in the local newspaper as Pet of the Week, but no one wanted a wild dog.

No one but Patricia Hollis of Kalamazoo, Michigan, that is. Patricia had a history of adopting hard-to-place pets. Some years before, she had regularly taken in homeless pets and found homes for them. A requirement for her adopters was to return pets they decided not to keep, and one returned pooch stayed with Patricia for thirteen years. When he passed away, she knew she wanted another dog and knew what kind: an Australian cattle dog, like a feral one she'd tamed during her days doing adoptions.

"I didn't want to go to the shelter because if I went in, I'd come out with fifteen dogs," Patricia says, half seriously. "Then my sister told me about Petfinder.com."

The Australian cattle dog in Pinckneyville was still running wild when Patricia first logged onto Petfinder.com, so he was not an option at that time. But she did see a photo of Carly, a cattle dog/whippet mix in Temperance, Michigan. Australian Cattle Dog (ACD) Rescue had pulled her from a municipal shelter in Tennessee with a full-blown case of distemper. ACD Rescue treated her, and she had survived, but she suffered neurological damage that resulted in almost continuous muscle spasms.

"I'm a social worker and I'm used to disabilities," Patricia says, "so that didn't throw me. I was more afraid someone would snap her up because she's such a beautiful dog." She needn't have worried. Carly's health issues scared off other potential adopters.

Patricia put the dog on a regimen of supplements and started exercising her regularly. "If you would look at her now, you wouldn't know she was the same dog."

About six months later, Patricia decided Carly needed a friend and, because she liked the whippet characteristics in Carly, she searched for whippets on Petfinder.com.

"I found R33 at Westmoreland County Shelter in Montross, Virginia. She was scheduled to be put to sleep in three days—road trip!" Patricia says. Her friend, Sonny Clark, agreed to join her on her adventure. It was a long drive, and the pair arrived in Montross after the shelter had closed. They managed to contact one of the staff, who agreed to open on Sunday to accommodate them.

Once the shelter finalized the adoption, Dog R33 became Bobbie Lee, so named because Robert E. Lee's birthplace was just down the road from the shelter. She was a whippet/hound mix.

Patricia now had two dogs, but she was still thinking about all the homeless dogs. "Legally in my community I could have three dogs, so I decided I should get another one."

That thought led her back to Petfinder.com and eventually to the feral dog, an Australian cattle dog/miniature pinscher mix, who had now been apprehended and had been at the shelter for about five months. He had acquired the name *Perry*, for Perry County where the humane society was located.

Patricia's friend, Sonny, once again accompanied her on her dog mission, and it took some determination to actually meet Perry. He was hiding in the back reaches of his cage, where he had spent most of the five months he had been there.

"I had to crawl all the way to the back of the kennel to get him out," Patricia recalls. "He was just like a block of wood, he was so terrified. He was pretty much that way for the entire ride home to Michigan.

"It was about midnight when we got back to Kalamazoo, and we went in and got Carly and took them to a neutral place," she says. "They barked a little and sniffed. Carly had to show him who was boss. Then they were fine."

Next Sonny brought Bobbie Lee out. Perry went right up to her as if to a long lost friend.

"He just kind of smooshed up against her," Patricia says, "and she licked him, and they've been bonded ever since. I call him her little pilot fish because wherever Bobbie goes, there's Perry right behind her."

On the trip back from Virginia, Sonny had bonded with Bobbie Lee, so he assumed responsibility for her, leaving Patricia's home one dog short of the legally mandated dog quota again.

This time around, Patricia wanted a different breed, so she typed in Australian shepherd. Up popped Johnny, listed by Three Sisters Rescue in Cincinnati. The photo of him was blurry, but his description said he was an Aussie mix, and his story touched Patricia. He had probably been chained up for most of his life because a veterinarian had to surgically remove a choke chain from around his neck after Three Sisters took him in. Patricia arranged with his foster family to meet in Bowling Green, Ohio.

When they arrived, "they opened their van door, and I thought, *'Oh my gosh, it's a hound dog.'* He was much bigger than I expected. He had Aussie coloring, but his hair was shorter than a cattle dog. He looked how an Australian shepherd might look with his fur shaved off. And he had a long nose." Even though he wasn't what she had hoped for, she decided to give him a try.

Carly, Perry, and Johnny settled into their "forever" home and Bobbie Lee visited at least twice a week. "Each and every one of the dogs fills a special niche in my life." Patricia continues, "I have children and grandchildren I adore, but I can't spend all my time with them; they have their own things to do. The dogs give me something to look forward to when I get up in the morning and something to come home to at night. I'm through adopting for now; my house is full." Patricia's full house is a winning hand.

Happiness Is a Big Bouvador

The Ellis kids were crying, and Mom and Dad, Jennifer and Brian Ellis, were just as sad as the children. They had just returned Max, a Bouvier des Flandres, to the animal placement group from which they'd adopted him hours earlier because he had attacked their old pooch, an aging Australian shepherd mix.

Their disappointment was magnified because they'd been looking for a dog for a long time. They were committed to adopting a homeless pet, either a Bouvier des Flandres, which Jennifer wanted, or a Labrador retriever, Brian's choice.

"My wife had grown up with a Bouvier," Brian says, "so she wanted another one because she knew they were protective, but nice. I wanted a Lab because we'd had one early in our marriage and she had been the perfect running partner."

The Ellises had four dogs, but three of them were small and weren't good running buddies, and the Australian shepherd didn't have much run left in him.

They began looking on Petfinder.com, looking for the perfect Lab or Bouvier. There weren't a lot of Bouviers listed on the Web site, so they were excited when one turned up not too far from their home in Titusville, Florida. They arranged to adopt him. The approval finally came on a Monday, and on Thursday they drove down to get Max.

"I had already been to the pet store and bought large dog things. I spent over two hundred dollars getting ready for him, so then Max doesn't work out, and we had all this stuff, even a fifty-pound bag of dog food, and I think, 'Oh my gosh, I've got to get *some* dog,' and I was desperate for a big one," remembers Brian.

Brian was cooking dinner on Friday when his wife, Jennifer, who was browsing on Petfinder.com, said, "Come over and look at this."

Brian was skeptical as he approached the computer, but this dog was different. Her description called her a *Bouvador*, fifty percent Bouvier and fifty percent Labrador. Jennifer and Brian wondered, *"Could this be the answer to our problem?"*

The potential answer to one problem seemed to beget another. Nakita, the dog staring back from the computer monitor, was in Divide, Colorado, a dot on the map west of Colorado Springs.

Brian got on the phone and called Teller County Regional Animal Shelter to ask if they still had Nakita. "They said she was still there and that her foster mom had just returned her because she was too big for them to keep. She was crying when she brought her in."

Brian was speaking to Toni Trujillo, the kennel manager at the shelter. She told him that Nakita was a beautiful dog and he should come and get her.

A bit of a problem, responded Brian, as he explained that he was in Florida. "They told me they didn't ship, so I got off the phone. But the more I thought about it, I decided to act. I got on the Internet and found a plane ticket for two hundred dollars. I was willing to take a chance. If there was a problem, I'd have a nice day in Denver. I called the airline to make sure there was room for Nakita on the return flight."

By eleven that night, Brian was making reservations on a 6:00 A.M. flight out of Orlando, about an hour from his home. He also reserved a rental car.

After about two hours of sleep, he embarked on his journey. "It was about seventy-five degrees when I left Orlando, and I'm wearing a tie-dyed shirt, shorts, and sandals. So as we're approaching Denver, it comes over the intercom that the present temperature in Denver is forty-one degrees. The plane lands, and I'm freezing."

He shivered his way to the rental car and headed south to Colorado Springs. There, he turned onto Route 24 past Pike's Peak.

"What a sight I was seeing," Brian recalls. "All of those snow-covered mountains looked magnificent. I hadn't seen snow in years. As I got closer to Divide, snow actually started to fall. I called my wife on the cell phone and said, 'You aren't going to believe this, but it's snowing.'"

Inside the Teller County Animal Shelter, the staff was getting ready to open when they heard someone knocking on the door.

"Here is this man in shorts and sandals," Toni says with a laugh. She opened the door and asked, "Are you the guy from Florida?"

Brian affirmed that he was, and Toni, thinking he was a little crazy, headed back to the kennels to get Nakita.

"She brings the dog out," Brian says, "and I am in awe. She was big and beautiful, weighing almost eighty-five pounds. She came over to me and began to lick me and wag her tail. I immediately fell in love with her and knew I had made the right decision about coming out to get her."

Nakita had the squarish head, sagging ears, and long, thick tail of a Labrador retriever. Her black hair was medium length, but at the moment she was not sporting the characteristic beard of a Bouvier.

Toni told Brian that Nakita's owner had turned her in because she had separation anxiety when they went to work and she dug up the yard. *Their loss,* thought Brian.

It was time to head back to Denver to catch his afternoon flight. He stopped in Colorado Springs to give Nakita a bath at a do-it-yourself facility, and he bought a giant kennel. It was so big that it would not fit into the rental car assembled, so he took it apart and stowed it in the back seat. Nakita rode beside him in the passenger seat, looking out—and shedding, as Bouviers do.

At the rental car facility, Brian apologized for the masses of dog hair that adorned the passenger seat. "It was a brand new car with only ten miles on it, now it was full of black dog hair," he says with a chuckle.

Brian and Nakita caught the rental agency's shuttle bus to the terminal, where an attendant helped him reassemble the kennel. Into it went Nakita, and then she had to go through special customs. They made it onto the plane five minutes before it took off.

When they taxied into Orlando, the passengers could hear a low "arf, arf, arf" from below.

"That's my dog," Brian said, with all the pride of a new father.

Brian had raced to the airport in his Volkswagen beetle that morning. After getting Nakita, he had realized that the bug wasn't big enough for the dog and the kennel, so he had called his wife to meet him at the airport. She and the kids met him with their minivan.

"The kids loved Nakita immediately," he recalls. "And she loved all the other dogs."

Brian had found his running buddy, and a swimming pal, as well. When the Florida heat proves to be too much on their outings, Nakita jumps into the Indian River, an inlet off the Atlantic, and swims with the manatees.

"It's amazing what I went through to find the perfect dog," he says. "If we hadn't looked on Petfinder, she'd have been sitting up there in Colorado and we would have never known about her."

Blessed Events

After seven years as a puppy "factory," the little white pug with the black ears couldn't have any more babies. Her owner, who operated a puppy mill, called an animal welfare group to come and take the dog off her hands.

Lisa-Ann McNeil of Maryland Pug Rescue responded to the call. "We have a unique relationship with the puppy millers in that we don't have to pay for the dogs. They are given to us when the breeder is retiring them or when something is wrong with them." In this particular dog's case, it was the latter.

"I wasn't sure what the problem was," Lisa-Ann recalls, "but it was clear she was in pain. I rushed her to the vet, and she had a bladder stone the size of a goose egg."

The stone was the largest the vet staff had seen in all their years of practice, and they estimated she'd had it for about a year. They began prepping her for surgery. Lisa-Ann stood by anxiously with tears welling in her eyes.

The vet tech reassured Lisa-Ann and said they needed a name for the dog.

"How about calling her Hope?" Lisa-Ann suggested.

The surgery went well, and Hope went to Lisa-Ann's to recover from the operation and from the traumas of the puppy mill, which would never be entirely erased. "She was painfully shy and always fearful of what a human hand would do, but it was clear she wanted affection. She immediately took to my pugs, and they all slept together. Potty training was an uphill battle, and when I first put her on a leash, she was like a fish at the end of a hook."

As Hope's recovery progressed, Lisa-Ann posted her on Petfinder.com. Her listing bore a little heart that identified her as a special needs pet, one that would require extra patience and understanding.

A special needs designation didn't daunt Jocelyn and Cliff Tichenor of Fredericksburg, Virginia, who logged onto Petfinder.com about the time Lisa-Ann posted Hope's description and photo. The Tichenors' beloved pug, Larry, had just passed away, and they were in shock.

Larry had been very special to them. Jocelyn had found him five years earlier when she was in North Carolina visiting a friend and saw him running loose in the woods. He obviously needed medical care, so Jocelyn gathered him up, whisked him to a local veterinarian, and got him fixed up. She placed a classified ad in the local newspaper, but no one called about a missing pug. By then she had named him *Larry*, and when she left for home, Larry ensconced himself beside her in the car.

"Larry and I hit it off right away," Cliff Tichenor remembers. "We were like best buddies."

He had five good years in his new home, but then he developed congestive heart failure, and eventually his kidneys began to fail.

"We realized how sick he was and that he just wanted to be let go," Cliff says. When the Tichenors took Larry to the vet to be put to sleep, Jocelyn collapsed in a tearful heap in the clinic's reception area. "Oh, God," she prayed aloud. "Please send us a little hope."

In the days that followed, the only way Jocelyn knew to resolve their overwhelming grief was to find another pug to help. She logged onto Petfinder.com and saw the listing for the special-needs pug that Lisa-Ann had rescued. She submitted an application, and Lisa-Ann set up an interview with the couple.

"When they told me how Jocelyn had found Larry," Lisa-Ann says, "well, people like that don't just come along every day."

When she called the Tichenors to tell them the news, Jocelyn answered the phone. Lisa-Ann told her they'd been approved to adopt "little Hope." Startled, Jocelyn asked, "What did you call her?"

"Well, her name is Hope, but since she only weighs seventeen pounds, we call her *Little Hope*."

Jocelyn remembered her prayer for "a little hope" at the veterinarians' office. The coincidence of the dog's name hadn't hit her until that moment. Now it registered. "God does answer prayers," Cliff says. "He sent us a little Hope."

"I feel blessed to have found the Tichenors," Lisa-Ann says. Hope is blessed as well.

Going the Distance

Someone had abandoned the black-and-white speckled pup in rural Idaho, and she took shelter in an unused commercial potato cellar. When the five-month-old Australian shepherd heard activity outside, she crawled out under the door to see what was going on.

Pam O'Hearn, who manages 3,000 acres for Idaho Fish and Game in the Menan, Idaho, area, had stopped at the spud cellar to let her dogs out of the truck to run the rest of the way home, about half a mile down the driveway. The abandoned pup enthusiastically joined them, racing down the driveway at a fast clip.

Pam might have been tempted to keep her, because she was "panda bear adorable" and personable as well, had the state not limited employees to two dogs in government housing. She and her husband, Jim, already had their quota.

She got on the phone and started calling the closest animal welfare organizations in the area, but to no avail. They were all filled to capacity. One of them suggested that she call Andi Elliott, president of the Humane Society of the Upper Valley in Idaho Falls.

Andi didn't have room either, but she was willing to work with Pam and Jim, who said they would gladly foster the pup if Andi would assist in placing her.

The arrangement was perfect. The O'Hearns gave the dog a temporary home, arranged for spaying and shots, and started housetraining her. The pup also had a chance to socialize with the couple's ferret, cats, two Labrador retrievers, and a friend's puppy, who was slightly younger.

"They would come over, and you want to talk about mayhem," Pam says with a laugh, recalling the madness. "Those puppies just had a ball."

She sent digital photos to Andi, who posted them on Petfinder. com. They showed the unique markings of the pup, whom Pam had named Roxie.

"I was not very hopeful about finding her a home because we have way too many unwanted Aussies, Border collies, and Labs in this area," Andi explains. Consequently, she was extremely pleased and somewhat surprised when, after only a week, Lois Bettini contacted her. What surprised her further was that the woman lived in Homer, Alaska, a small town on Alaska Bay.

Lois and her husband, Doug Schwiesow, wanted a dog that would fit into their active lifestyle, and the more Doug learned about the traits of Australian shepherds, the more he thought the breed would be the perfect match. Lois was so dog starved, she says, that she would have gone along with whatever Doug wanted. They began searching on Petfinder.com after they learned about the site from a friend in Utah who was involved in Border collie placement.

"There aren't many Aussies in Alaska," says Lois, "so we took our friend's advice and looked in Utah and Idaho, where there seem be a lot of them needing homes." That led them to Roxie.

As Andi interviewed Lois, she realized this was going to be a dream placement for Roxie. She would live on ten acres and go running, fishing, and cross-country skiing with her pet parents, just the kind of family an energetic Aussie needed.

Of course, there was the matter of transport. Homer was about 2000 miles from Idaho Falls. Lois didn't want Roxie to travel on an airplane alone, so Andi's husband, John stepped in to help get the pooch to Alaska.

During a layover in Salt Lake City, John called Andi from the airport and complained that the authorities wouldn't let him take Roxie out of her crate, even though it was going to be a wait of several hours.

Andi, in best animal-advocate fashion, told John to start at the bottom and work his way to the top—whatever it took—to get that dog out during the layover.

When he called back a while later, he reported that he had taken her advice and had succeeded. He and Roxie were walking around the airport as he spoke.

Roxie settled right into her new home, and her new family quickly found that she lived up to an Aussie's reputation as a shepherd. "If you kick a soccer ball, she goes to get it and herds it back to you," Lois says. "If you kick three, she gets them all together. She makes sure that anything that is part of a group, stays with the group—kids, friends, bikes." She also herds the family's three ducks—although they also like to herd her.

Roxie is energetic and enthusiastic. Beyond that, she brings joy to her new family.

Says Lois, "She is a special dog and those who rescued her and helped us adopt her are truly special people."

Tammy's Hero

Tammy Parker of Shelbyville, Tennessee, leaned against the wall of the shower stall. Her breath came in short gasps as she began to hyperventilate. She had taken off her oxygen tube to shower, and now she was about to pass out, her life-giving oxygen out of reach.

"Mama," she gasped, but her mother, with whom she lived, was relaxing on the back porch and couldn't hear her cries for help.

Tammy was about as desperate at that moment as she had been since she became ill in 1998. Her doctor told her she had stage four Hodgkin's lymphoma. In the next few years, she underwent four operations and a stem cell transplant that wiped out her immune system. She was so susceptible to any virus that happened by that she was housebound during the winters, and even then spent much of the time sick and in bed. When she did get out, she often used a wheelchair, and an oxygen tank became a necessity.

Her disease went into remission in July 2004, but Tammy remained depressed both physically and mentally. "I just needed something to get up for," she says. "I was looking for a reason to live."

Tammy decided the *something* might be a dog. "I wanted a small dog that wouldn't trigger my asthma, and one day I got lucky and found Petfinder while surfing on the Web. I just happened to see this Shih Tzu as I was scrolling through a list of pets in my area. He just cried out to me."

The little black-and-white dog was named *Ozzo*, and his owners had relinquished him to Rock N Acres Animal Rescue. "We get a lot of owner surrenders," explains Sherry Ford, who started the rescue. "Ozzo's family didn't want him because he had an eye condition and they didn't want to bother with treating it."

He also had come into Sherry's care matted and unkempt because the owners had been generally negligent of the little guy's upkeep. Sherry asked her mother, Mary Ford, to foster Ozzo while she sought a permanent placement for him.

Although small dogs were usually in high demand, Ozzo's eye condition and his age worked against him. He was virtually blind and was three to four years old.

Neither fact deterred Tammy. "Yes, he had some health problems, but so did I."

She applied to adopt him, but when she told the rescue she didn't have a fenced yard, they were hesitant. She assured them that she was home all the time and would be a devoted "mom."

"I called Mary every day, telling her I wanted him," Tammy recalls. "I said I need him, and it looks as if he needs me, too."

Finally, one Saturday, she told her mother, "I've given up. I don't want a dog. I don't want anything."

Tammy's persistence, however, had paid off. The following Monday, Mary called and said Tammy could adopt Ozzo. Her spirits soared, and she felt better than she had in years.

On Tuesday, she made the trip and fell in love with the dog all over again. She promptly changed his name to Ozzie.

Once back home, Ozzie quickly bonded with his new owner and stayed right by her side. Ozzie's new veterinarian diagnosed his eye condition as conjunctivitis, and Tammy began treating him every day, and soon much of his vision came back.

She threw a birthday party for him and invited relatives and their eleven dogs. The pooches wore colorful kerchiefs she had made, and they each sported a party hat.

Tammy, who couldn't drive during the worst of her illness, began to venture out more and got a little car seat for Ozzie. Once a month he went to the veterinarian for an allergy shot, and he regularly visited the groomer. Well-coifed and handsome, Ozzie had all the earmarks of a beloved pet.

Then came the day in the shower. As Tammy leaned against the wall of the shower stall, feeling desperate, the bathroom door moved a bit as Ozzie pushed his way in. He had heard Tammy's weak cries for help.

"Ozzie, get Nannie," Tammy gasped.

The little dog hurried through the house and to the back door. He knew Tammy was in trouble. He had never barked before, but now he barked and barked, getting Mom's attention. She ran in to assist her daughter. Ozzie scampered along just to make sure Tammy was okay.

"I have no doubt that he saved my life that day," Tammy says. The formerly unwanted pooch was a hero.

From 238 to No. 1

E ven in the dog world, society puts stock in youth and good
looks. So is there a place for a five-year-old hairless dog with
no name? This dog started out with just a number, 238. It was
tattooed on her inner thigh as a means of identification at the
Missouri puppy mill where she was born and repeatedly bred.

When law enforcement officers raided the mill and shut it
down, they shipped the dogs to breed-specific rescue groups that
were willing to find homes for them. Number 238, along with
others, went to Forgotten Friends, an animal welfare organization based in Plant City, Florida. Life was looking better for the
pooch.

Things got even better when Andrea and Robert Potts, who
were living in Orlando, decided to adopt a dog after one of theirs
had passed away. They still had one pooch, a mini-dachshund
named Gator, but they felt he needed company. Andrea found
an online breed selector that helped people figure out what kind

of dog would be a good match for them. The selector suggested a Chinese crested dog.

Andrea had never even heard of the breed, and when she saw a photo of one, she had to laugh aloud. A pooch that resembled a miniature naked horse with an unruly topknot that rivaled Cosmo Kramer's hair stared back at her from her computer monitor.

Ugliness didn't stop Andrea. She logged onto Petfinder.com and entered *Chinese crested* in the search box. She also entered *adult* because she knew that mature dogs have the hardest time finding homes. Though the Chinese crested breed is unusual, one popped up on the monitor. Black spots dappled its almost white skin. "It looked like a tiny Dalmatian," Andrea remembers, which seemed to her like fate stepping in because the dog she'd lost had been a Dalmatian.

She e-mailed the placement group, and they interviewed her about her home situation. When she told them about Gator, they said the spotted dog wouldn't be a good choice because he didn't do well with other pooches. As an alternative, they e-mailed her a photo of another dog, which happened to be Number 238, renamed Fuji. The Forgotten Friends volunteer admitted that Fuji wasn't as attractive as Andrea's first choice, but said she was a wonderful dog.

"She looked like a pig with a wig," Andrea said, "and one snaggletooth jutted out of her mouth. But I trusted the organization's advice and told them I would love to meet her."

A volunteer brought her to visit, and Andrea got her first look at the dog in the flesh, literally. Fuji's pale, ultra-soft hairless skin was dotted with age spots and freckles. When Andrea touched her it was reminiscent of putting her hands on a hot water bottle. Andrea fell instantly in love with the dog who would never win any beauty contests. With the adoption complete, Andrea changed the little dog's name. "I figured people wouldn't know what she was in the first place, so I thought a very girlie name would at least let them know she was a girl dog." Fuji became Lucy. "My husband came up with Lucille Bald, which is so-o-o-o appropriate."

It was quite true that people didn't know what to make of this dog. "They ask me: Is she sick? Is something wrong with her? Do you cut her hair like that? It took my husband three months before he'd hug her because she felt so weird," Andrea says with a laugh. "But she has completely won him over. Our next dog will probably be a Chinese crested."

Lucy had come through her puppy mill experience fairly unscathed psychologically, although she does show odd behaviors.

"You know how most dogs turn around several times before they lie down?" Andrea asks. "We counted over forty turns before she settled down. It's as if she gets stuck. I think it comes from being in a confined area for so long."

Another characteristic is her voraciousness at feeding time. "She acts as if she's afraid she won't get her next meal," says Andrea. She speculates that the breeders withheld food from her at the puppy mill. At the very least, she may have had to fight for her share.

These few quirks aside, Lucy is basically calm and amiable. Andrea thought her personality made her a perfect candidate to visit people in nursing homes, so she signed her up with Pet Pals, a volunteer organization whose members take their pets to visit Alzheimer's patients. Andrea places Lucy in a patient's lap, and the little pooch sits quietly while the patient holds her.

"Often the residents have had dogs," Andrea says, "and they like to talk about them."

The former puppy mill dog was really blossoming, so when Andrea saw a dog contest announced in the Orlando Sentinel, she decided to move Lucy into the limelight. This wasn't just any dog contest; Andrea and Robert thought Lucy had a darn good chance of winning "Orlando's Ugliest Dog" contest. They signed her up, and sure enough, Lucy walked away with the prize when readers voted her first place.

"We were very proud," Andrea says. "People tell us how lucky Lucy was to have found us, but I feel that we were the lucky ones. She is a true Petfinder.com success story."

Home Again

Annie Wilson couldn't help but be disappointed. She knew the dog that she and her husband Kody had adopted would have a period of adjustment, but Marley hadn't come out of her crate for two days. When they'd first seen her at a foster home, the dog had trembled and kept her tail between her legs, but Annie had fully hoped that she would quickly blossom. So far, it hadn't happened.

The Wilsons found Marley listed on Petfinder.com by Save A Dog Today, an animal placement organization based in Lakehead, California. She was an English Staffordshire terrier and was approximately one year old. Volunteers had plucked her from a shelter, where she had been held after being picked up on the streets.

Annie and Kody had applied to adopt her, and after they'd sent photos of their home and yard to Save A Dog Today and filled out the adoption applications, they were chosen to be Marley's "parents."

They had set out for Redding, California, where Marley was being fostered, about 700 miles south of their home in Vancouver, Washington. Because of the distance, they hoped the decision was a good one; otherwise it would be a long and fruitless trip.

When they first laid eyes on Marley, shaking and scared, their hearts said it had been the right thing to do. "We fell in love with this poor little girl," Annie says.

They loaded Marley into her crate in the back of their station wagon, said their goodbyes to her foster mom, and headed home.

The journey wasn't idyllic. During the eleven-hour ride, Marley shook and panted the whole way. "I tried to give her treats and pets, and we talked to her non-stop," Annie recalls. They even took their socks off and put them in her crate to acclimate her to their scent, but nothing seemed to pacify Marley.

"When we stopped at a rest area for her to go potty, she was obviously miserable," Annie remembers sadly. "She hated the leash. She hated the walk. She hated us. We were so heartbroken that she was so sad and scared. It was very hard to see her like that." In spite of their earlier confidence, they couldn't help but wonder if they had made a big mistake.

"When we got home, we picked her up and took her into the house," Annie says. "She lay in her bed in the corner with a look of pure panic and fear in her eyes." It was disheartening. This went on for about a week.

"Then one night Marley woke me at about 2:30 A.M. and wanted to go out to potty," Annie relates. "It was pouring rain, about forty-five degrees, but I took her out. To my surprise, she wanted to play. It was as if she had known me for a lifetime. I got soaking wet in my pajamas, but I didn't care. Marley was playing."

Annie stayed outside with Marley until 6:30 A.M. when it was time to get ready for work. Her husband, just rousing from sleep as she re-entered the house, was startled to see his bedraggled wife with a look of pure joy on her face. Annie exclaimed, "Honey, she played with me."

That was the first turning point in Marley's relationship with her new family.

Because Marley was a stray, no one knew what had befallen her during her first year. As the days passed, it became apparent to the Wilsons that someone had abused her. She panicked at the sight of ropes, and the leash scared her. Her tail had obviously been broken and not been taken care of.

"It really took a good six months before she really warmed up to us," Annie says. "She began lying with us on the couch with her head on our laps, and she gave us kisses, and she bounced up and down when she got excited." Marley loved her backyard, and the squirrels and raccoons offered lots of excitement. But she was still a dog wrought with anxiety.

Her anxiety reached crisis proportions when one December day a neighbor shot off some firecrackers. Marley, who was in the backyard, apparently found a hole under the fence and ran away in a panic.

"When I discovered she was gone, I felt I had lost a child," Annie says.

Marley had become the light of their lives. She had filled the couple with a love they didn't know existed, deep and unconditional, and now she was missing. It was almost unbearable.

"I went to the humane society three times a day and put up about a thousand flyers," Annie says. "I'd go home and sleep then go out looking again."

On the fifth day, Annie got a call from a woman who said she had seen one of the flyers and that she had Marley. Annie and Kody were overjoyed.

As it turned out, Marley had been in the caller's backyard since she had disappeared, but the woman and her husband had been out of town and their dog sitter was afraid to let Marley in. She had, however, fed her.

When the couple returned from their trip, they welcomed her into the house and began looking for her owners. The woman had called the humane society and had also taken Marley to a veterinary clinic to see if she was microchipped. Both locations had flyers posted or had been contacted, but no one put two and two together and alerted Annie. The caller's husband, however, noticed a flyer posted in a convenience store window while he waited in the car for his wife at the vet's office.

Annie and Kody hurried over to the couple's house, about six blocks from their home.

"When we arrived," Annie says, "I could see Marley through the crack in the door and I just lost it. I started crying, and my husband was crying—and he's not the crying type. Once we went in, Marley was all over us. She was so excited to see us."

Annie explained how they had adopted her.

Her words and Marley's reaction reassured the people. They too felt the dog had once been abused and were prepared to call the humane society to come and get her if the dog showed any reluctance about going with the Wilsons.

"We were so relieved to have her back," Annie says. "We all stayed home together and didn't leave the house for about a week. I didn't even go to work. Since then, she has been so much more bonded with us and is stronger emotionally overall. She's more of a regular dog now. It's as if she knew we had come to get her and it meant she could trust us."

This time, Marley was really home.

Poodle Fever

Sandy Blackburn had a serious case of poodle fever. A dog groomer, she worked on lots of breeds, but her competitive streak made her want to get creative in her buzzing and clipping.

"Standard poodles have an air about them," says Sandy. "They're very elegant, and I said to myself, I need a poodle."

She logged onto Petfinder.com, and up came "this black standard. She was the most pitiful thing I'd ever seen. Her head was hanging down, and she looked depressed. She weighed forty-five pounds and had been shaved naked."

Sandy couldn't quit thinking about the seven-year-old dog. "Her story said she was a product of a divorce," Sandy relates. "The guy had put her in his backyard and let her starve. He had a yard sale, and a groomer happened to go to it and said something about the poodle. The man said, 'If you want her, you can have her.'" The woman turned the dog over to Plano Zoo, a small animal placement group in Plano, Texas, and she was placed in a foster home.

The problem was that the dog, Katy, was in Texas and Sandy lived in Attica, Indiana. "I called them after I saw Katy's picture, and the foster 'mom' said she thought she could find her a home in Texas. So I thought, 'Oh fine. I'll just give up on it.'"

About that time, Sandy saw an "Animal Cops" show about a dog that had been starved. "Katy kept popping into my mind. I couldn't stop thinking about her."

Sandy called the animal placement group again and talked them into doing a long distance adoption.

It was July, too hot to fly Katy to her new home, so Sandy started trying to arrange transport. She finally managed to get a commitment from someone to drive Katy to Muskogee, Oklahoma, and another person to do a leg from St. Louis. The middle of the trip proved impossible to fill, so Sandy packed up for a trip to Muskogee.

Sandy's husband, Tim, didn't seem enthusiastic about this new dog, but she packed a bag for him, just in case. When she and her two sons, four-year-old Drew and one-year-old Lane, were heading out the door, Tim came out and hopped into the driver's seat.

"He was interested in Katy, too," says a pleased Sandy.

They made a beeline for Muskogee, but she had done some planning and had mapped out a few pet-friendly stops along the way home. One was a cave in Missouri that allowed dogs because a dog had discovered it, according to Sandy.

"I have this picture from that day in the cave with forty strangers prominently displayed on my wall," she says. The strangers are in a wagon being hauled by a Jeep, but the Blackburns are in the Jeep itself because they were accompanied by a dog, albeit a scrawny, pathetic-looking one.

"The worst thing about the cave trip was how awful Katy looked. I wanted to say, 'She's a rescue. I didn't do this to her,'" Sandy remembers.

Every time the family took a break at a rest stop, people stared. It made Sandy all the more eager to get her home and spruced up.

"We got there about two o'clock in the morning, and I got a second wind and buzzed her all down and bathed her," she says.

Katy met her new "sister," Brittany, a collie who was the spitting image of Lassie. The two dogs hit it off and have never butted heads on anything, according to Sandy.

"We had a tornado come through and the tornado sirens were going off. I thought we'd better hit the ditch," Sandy says. "I got everyone down to the basement. The dogs had never used stairs before in their lives. They're saying, 'What is this?' and I'm dragging them down there. Brittany kept looking up the stairs." When it was over, she went up with everybody, but Katy stayed at the bottom pacing.

"Oh criminy," Sandy thought. *"She doesn't know how to get back up them now."*

Brittany saw Katy's distress, went down, nudged her side, and walked back up the stairs with her. "Anybody who doesn't believe animals communicate with each other should have seen them."

Not long after she had buzzed off all of Katy's hair she learned that the American Grooming Show in Chicago had brought back their creative grooming competition. It was just the sort of event that inspired Sandy's poodle fever.

"And I had just shaved my dog," she recalls, her voice rising. "I had no hair to work with. I had six weeks, so I'm feeding her eggs and brushing her—anything to stimulate hair growth. I'm thinking, '*What can I do with short hair?*' I came up with turning her into a tree."

Sandy shaved the shapes of leaves into her short coat, added a bird's nest in her top knot and made her tail into a beehive with fake bees hovering around it. Sandy dressed like a birdwatcher. They walked away with second place.

Sandy liked to dress Katy up for holidays. She garnered lots of attention on Halloween when she went out with the Blackburn boys, who were dressed like Spiderman and Superman. Katy was The Hulk.

Sandy loaned Katy to one of her grooming clients to teach her Welsh terrier some manners. The woman was amazed at how a large dog like Katy could be so graceful and how she could bounce around in a house full of antiques and never knock down a thing.

But Katy still wasn't all foo-foo. "She belches like a sailor," Sandy says with a laugh. One day Sandy was on the phone, and Katy, standing nearby, let out a big burp. Sandy found herself explaining to the person on the other end of the line, "Uh, that wasn't me; it was my dog."

Sandy came up with the idea of having a fun dog show at a nursing home each year. She suggested it to the activities director, who liked the idea. People brought in their dogs and participated in contests like "longest tail" and "owner look-alike." Katy showed off a trick Sandy taught her.

"I have her sit, gimme five, then I make her lie down," Sandy says. "Then I ask her, 'Katy, would you rather be married or dead?' She rolls over and plays dead and stays there." It never fails to get big laughs from the residents and staff.

"I've never met a rescued pet I didn't adore," Sandy says enthusiastically. "They seem so glad they finally have a 'forever' home that they are the most obedient, loving, sweetest animals on earth. We love Katy with all of our hearts and know God brought us together."

Gentle Guardian

Tara Miller, a volunteer at the Humane Society in Frisco, Texas, had a particular interest in the "bully" breeds, like American pit bull terriers, bull terriers, and English bulldogs. When one of the staff at an animal shelter in Dallas called to alert her that a pit bull had come into their facility, she and Lisa Lipton, another volunteer, headed to the shelter to meet him.

A yellow Labrador retriever watched with interest as Tara took the pit out of its run to see if he had the temperament to be a good pet. Animal control, she later learned, had picked up the Lab as a stray when he and a female dog were nosing through some trash, looking for food.

As Tara returned the pit to his kennel, the Lab honed in on Tara. "I tested several other dogs while I was there, and every time I'd go by this Lab to get another dog, he would just be sitting there, watching."

He wasn't much to look at, she admits. "His ears didn't match and his feet worked faster than his body. There was really nothing outstanding about him." Except he kept watching, and in his look, she saw something special and, on a whim, decided to test him.

"He flew through the temperament test," she says. "I picked him up. I turned him upside down. I pulled his tail. I flipped his ears inside out. I screamed and ran toward him saying, 'Puppy, puppy, puppy,' like a kid would, and he just sat there like, 'Oh, this is so cool.' He loved it."

Tara didn't pull any other dogs out of the shelter that day, but she made arrangements to 'spring' the Lab. She convinced Lisa to keep him for a few days while she placed some other foster dogs to make room for him at her home. Lisa named him Leo because, she says, "He reminded me of a lion with his long curving tail. He was such a gentle giant."

When Tara had made room, Leo moved to her house. He tested positive for heartworms, but she postponed treatment while she got him up to weight. "He was pretty thin at first, and I didn't want to make him sicker."

Tara, who trains assistance dogs, started teaching Leo basic obedience, and because he trained easily and would do anything to please her, it looked as if he was destined to be an assistance dog. Then his destiny changed.

During his heartworm treatment, Lisa had to keep Leo quiet. To alleviate his boredom, she placed his kennel in a spot where he could see outside. She noticed that when Leo saw children passing by or riding their bikes, he would start 'talking' like Scooby Doo. He would continue for about ten minutes after the kids had disappeared.

To make him happy, "I finally gave up and just walked him outside when the neighborhood kids were out," she recalls. "I told them he was sick and had to remain quiet. So they sat down on the sidewalk, and Leo got to lie next to them. He was asleep within minutes. He was in pure bliss around kids."

By then she had posted his description and photo on Petfinder. com, and several people expressed interest. "Some wanted him to be an outside dog," she says, "others wanted a jogging partner." No one, however, was quite right for Leo, in Tara's estimation, because none of them had children. She went online and revised his description on Petfinder: Must be in a family with children.

About that time Jennifer Watkins, who as it turned out lived just down the road from Tara Miller, had decided her two young children, Gage and Keely, were ready for a dog. "We wanted a large dog that liked children and cats," Jennifer explains. "House-trained was a plus because I was training my two-year-old and I didn't want to potty train a dog and a toddler at the same time." When she asked five-year-old Gage what he wanted in a dog, he simply said, "One that plays."

She came upon Leo's listing, and he sounded perfect to Jennifer. When they met Leo, it was a match, and the Watkins family took him home.

"He is so gentle with the children," says Jennifer. "They climb all over him, giving him love, and he just eats up the attention. He watches over them better than I can at times."

One day when she was gardening in the front yard, little Keely toddled to the curb while Jennifer was momentarily distracted. When she looked up, she was horrified to see that her little girl was about to step into the street. Before Jennifer could even react, Leo was there. He planted himself between Keely and the street and would not let her pass. This loving eighty-pound guardian was determined to keep Keely out of harm's way.

"I didn't train him to do that," Tara Miller said. "Leo is just one of those dogs who is instinctively protective."

Another time, the family left Leo home alone, and a strong wind blew the front door open. Some dogs would have headed out into the neighborhood to explore. Not Leo. He plopped down at the doorway and guarded.

The neighbor, knowing the family was gone and noticing the door standing open, came over to shut it. Leo warned him off by howling and barking. As soon as the family returned, Leo was relieved of duty and ran over to give the neighbor a friendly kiss.

"I could hardly believe it," Jennifer says, "because Leo had never shown an ounce of aggression, even to strangers. I knew, though, he was simply keeping us safe."

Tara Miller agrees. "I knew there was something special about Leo from the first time I saw him at that shelter. "You can walk by a hundred dogs, but then you see that special one—that was Leo."

In the Nick of Time

Holly and Kenny Todd, who lived in San Jose, California, at the time, came home from vacation to find their pet sitter had let their cat, Oscar, escape. Kenny walked the neighborhood, talking to people and distributing flyers to every door in a two-mile radius to no avail. Holly visited the local humane society nightly to see if anyone had turned Oscar in.

"A very kind volunteer at the shelter asked me if I had visited Petfinder.com," says Holly. "She explained that shelters and rescues all over the area post photos of animals on it and that maybe I could find Oscar there."

Holly hurried home and logged on, armed with a ray of hope. She poured over countless photos day after day, but no Oscar. The Todds never did find their beloved cat.

To take her mind off of Oscar, Holly began looking at homeless dogs on Petfinder.com. "Even before Oscar disappeared, I'd been wanting a dog and even knew what breed. Kenny had an

Australian cattle dog before we married and said if he ever got another dog, it would be a cattle dog."

She typed in her search terms and entered her zip code. The computer did its magic, and up came the photo of A572263, a white cattle dog "covered with red polka dots," according to Holly. She was at the South Los Angeles Animal Shelter.

"The picture was a profile shot," Holly recalls. "She was sitting really tall and staring straight ahead, very alert. It was as if she was paying attention to someone. She looked smart."

Holly read the shelter's home page and realized that, in the overcrowded city facility, the dog's days were numbered unless someone adopted her.

Kenny came into the room and glanced over her shoulder. "Nice dog," he commented. With a heavy heart, Holly told him about the shelter's euthanasia policy.

He asked if the shelter was open the following day, which surprised Holly. Was Kenny thinking of driving to L.A. to adopt the dog?

Holly checked the Web site and learned that the shelter did indeed have Sunday hours.

Then Kenny wondered aloud if the dog was still there. Perhaps the records hadn't been updated. His question prompted Holly to get on the phone, but she had no luck reaching the shelter. The line remained busy.

But neither of them could get the dog off their minds.

Finally Kenny said, "There's something about that dog. We can't just leave her there to die."

Within an hour, Holly and Kenny were packed and on the road. They got to L.A. late and spent the night in a motel.

"I woke up at eight, wide awake and ready to pick up my dog," Holly says. "One problem—the shelter didn't open until eleven." Three hours to go. The couple headed for a pet store to buy supplies for the dog they weren't even sure was still alive.

That fear grew when they arrived at the shelter and reached the front desk.

"Hmm," the woman there said as she pulled up the number of the dog. "This dog came in three weeks ago. I doubt she's still here."

Holly's heart sank. "Well," the woman continued, still perusing her records, "she may still be here. Go through those doors and ask to go to Kennel 13."

The couple complied eagerly.

The man at the next desk scratched his head. "I don't think she's here. I'm pretty sure she went yesterday morning. Let me call someone." He raised a phone to his ear while Holly worried over what he meant by "went."

"Yeah, A572263," the man said into the phone. "She's gone right? . . . Kennel 12? . . . Okay . . . Yeah, I have someone who wants to see her."

Holly's spirits rose. Apparently A572263 was still there.

The man put down the receiver and directed the Todds down a corridor lined with kennels.

"Dogs and more dogs and more dogs, all on top of each other," Holly recalls sadly, describing what she saw. "Five or six animals sharing a small space. Some were pacing; others were wrestling, most were barking or crying."

As they passed by, Holly mumbled to Kenny that if the dog they'd come for wasn't there, they were going to adopt another one of these pooches. They weren't going home empty handed when so many needed homes.

They arrived in front of Kennel 12. Holly took a deep breath and looked in. The kennel was empty.

Crestfallen, she and Kenny retraced their steps back to the desk and told the man the dog wasn't there. A female shelter worker who was standing there explained that the kennels had an inside and outside area. Sometimes the dogs got stuck on the other side, she said.

Down the corridor the couple went again, following the worker back to the kennels. They looked into a restricted area.

"We saw her with the other dogs," Holly says, "and they were biting and bullying her."

The woman brought the dog, prancing and smiling, into the hallway on a leash.

"I bent down and she jumped in my lap and licked me in the face," remembers Holly. "It was as if she knew she was getting sprung. It was all I could do not to burst into tears."

The dog was about eight months old, very skinny, and covered with bite marks. Holly learned that the pup had been picked up as a stray.

Holly and Kenny led her back to the desk to fill out the paperwork to adopt her. The volunteer who had posted her on

Petfinder.com was standing there and explained that the dog had been there three weeks, far beyond the norm, because her personality made her a shelter favorite. Each time her number came up, the staff rallied behind her to make space and keep her alive.

Time had run out, though, because the pup had developed a cough. The volunteer had been trying to find an animal placement group that would take her out of the shelter, but her search had been unsuccessful.

"She wouldn't have been here tomorrow," the woman said. "You were just in the nick of time."

The Todds had already chosen a name for their new "kid": Kona.

"There are times when I'll be hanging out with her in the backyard on a warm breezy day," Holly says, "and she'll lean against me and nuzzle under my chin, just like she did that first time I saw her. I know she's saying *thank you*. But what I want her to know is how much she has given to us. We may have saved her life, but she has made our lives so much richer."

Quite a Dandy

Too aggressive. Untrained. Those were the kinds of descriptors Brandy's first owners leveled against him. They kept the feisty two-year-old Pomeranian cooped up all day in a crate, and then wondered why he barked constantly. Nothing he did was right.

Finally, the owners put the little pooch in the car and took him for a ride—right to the overcrowded county animal shelter where they relinquished him, knowing full well that if he wasn't adopted he would be put to sleep.

Of course, they probably believed he would find a new home. They knew how irresistible poms were. And they were right. A new family arrived on the scene quickly.

Almost as quickly, he was returned. Once, twice. *Aggressive. Untrainable.* The behaviors tainted his chance for a "forever" home, and no one was willing to take the time to rehabilitate the little guy.

In spite of the dog's reputation, one staff member at the shelter thought he was sweet and deserved still another chance, and when he ended up on the short list for euthanasia, she called Karen Kaeumlen of Adopt-a-Buddy, a New Jersey animal welfare organization. Karen went into action and listed him on Petfinder.com.

Her description didn't leave anything unsaid, and when Hannah McCullough, of Franklinville, New Jersey, read it she figured no one would want this dog. She showed his photo and story to her husband, Jack.

"I don't think there's anyone but me who would adopt him," she said.

Hannah was at a good place in her life to adopt a dog. She had been a self-described cat person—and the couple had a dozen or so cats to prove it. "I have always loved all animals, but thought dogs needed more individual attention."

She had traveled on the job for fifteen years, but had recently made a change and all her sales calls would be local. That meant she could devote time to a dog, and as if by fate, right then this dog that needed her desperately appeared on Petfinder.com.

Hannah contacted Karen, who agreed to do a cat-test before going any further. Any McCullough dog had to get along with the resident cats. Brandy passed the test, and Hannah went ahead with the adoption.

"It's incredible that his original write-up said he was so bad because he is such a love bug," Hannah says. "Yes, he did bark and chase the cats at first, but I kept him on-leash in the house and in the yard until he became adjusted to them, and they to him. It took about two weeks. Once they all knew they were part of the same family, they got along great.

"The only vaguely aggressive behavior we had with him was when he barked, jumped, and spun around uncontrollably if a car, bicycle, or another dog passed us during his walks."

Using treats, she learned to redirect his attention away from whatever was causing him to bark and soon modified his behavior.

The McCulloughs, who changed Brandy's name to Dandy, believed that one of his previous owners had abused him because "he freaked out when Jack brought out the flyswatter to hit a fly. He came charging out at the flyswatter, barking and attacking it, growling and gnawing at it," Hannah relates.

Rather than blaming the dog, the couple saw this as a problem to be solved and began desensitizing him to the flyswatter by stroking him gently with it. He soon learned to ignore it.

"We took him everywhere," she recalls. "Kids would come up and pet him and pull at his ears, and he was always an angel." His behavior was so counter to what his previous owners had reported that Hannah began to think that people made up stories to justify giving up their pets.

"Wherever we went people would ask where we found such a beautiful, affectionate dog—and I would say 'at the animal shelter.' I passed out little business cards I printed up for Dandy that told where he came from. Several of my neighbors adopted dogs from the shelter after meeting Dandy, and there's no telling how many strangers did."

Dandy had become a goodwill ambassador for shelter dogs.

Meanwhile, Hannah spotted another dog, a sheltie/pom mix named Frankie, on Petfinder.com who needed her.

"A kid had purchased him at a pet store," Hannah says, "and then tied him to a tree in the backyard for three years. When the

boy went into the military, his parents said he'd have to get rid of the dog. The boy gave him to a lady he knew, who knew someone in S.T.A.R.T.," an animal welfare group based in Little Falls, New Jersey. They posted him on Petfinder.

Hannah recalled that his description said something like, "If you are somebody who can have a small dog that doesn't like to be picked up, then Frankie might be the dog for you." With a laugh, Hannah says, "That was code for 'he may bite you.'"

Once again, Hannah figured this dog wouldn't find a home unless she and Jack gave him one.

No doubt about it, Frankie had socialization issues. "We'd walk down the street and he'd be lunging, snarling, barking, and carrying on," Hannah remembers. "I couldn't talk to anyone."

She signed him up for obedience classes, and the trainer worked specifically on getting Frankie to accept strangers. "People in the class were given treats to drop in front of him as they passed. It progressed to holding a treat and giving it to him. He made an amazing transformation. We go down the street now and people can come up and he sits quietly or goes into a down-stay position."

Hannah and Jack now had two dogs no one had wanted, but she kept browsing on Petfinder.com. It was just a matter of time until she saw another needy pet she couldn't resist.

That dog was another pom named Peanut. The West Jersey Animal Shelter had plucked the scrawny senior right off the streets. His raggedy coat was mangy, and rotten teeth lined his mouth.

"These are the dogs I pick," Hannah says. "Let me have that old dog with the bad teeth. Or how about the one that snarls?"

Peanut snarled to let his new family know that when it came to food, he was a force to be reckoned with.

"If one of the cats or dogs walks by," Hannah says, "he starts to snarl and you can see his teeth. He looks like a small possum." She liked to treat the dogs to a dog biscuit from time to time. "He can't eat them," she says. He takes his and hides it in his pillow.

"Frankie likes to tease the others. He'll put his dog biscuit down, then he'll sleep about a foot away from it with one eye open, just daring them to try to take it. They're just so much fun.

"They follow me everywhere," Hannah continues. "I tell Jack they're my little posse. Who would want any of them? But, boy, are they special. They are the joy of our lives."

Hannah went on to found Faithful Friends Pet Rescue and joined Petfinder.com to facilitate finding homes for pets she rescued. Dandy, as it turned out, was not the only dandy in the McCullough household. Hannah herself qualified.

Called to Service

Mabel sneezed, then wiped her nose. No one said, "Bless you" or "Gesundheit," but everyone laughed, which was perfectly okay with her, and it made Mabel's owner, Beth Malekoff of Pittstown, New Jersey, especially proud.

Beth had taken the golden Labrador retriever through lots of training—basic obedience, Canine Good Citizen, pet-assisted therapy, and pet tricks—and Mabel had become a certified therapy dog. The laughter from these elderly people in a nursing home was her reward.

"Some of them had had pets at home and had to leave them to go into the nursing home," explains Beth. "Mabel helps them feel better."

Perhaps even more rewarding than their work with the elderly was the volunteer work Beth and Mabel did at St. Joseph's Children's Hospital in Paterson, New Jersey. Besides making the children laugh with her tricks, Mabel reassured them by example as they "doctored" her with toy instruments and the staff hooked her up to heart monitors and IVs.

"She just stayed still and let them do whatever they needed to," Beth says. "We tried to make whatever they would be going through easier for them."

For her volunteer work, Mabel was inducted into the New Jersey Veterinary Medical Association/Ralston-Purina Hall of Fame in 2001. Mabel's induction as a therapy pet was all the more touching because less than two years earlier she was at Cumberland County SPCA in Vineland, New Jersey, and her future was uncertain.

Beth saw Mabel on Petfinder.com and made the two-and-a-half-hour trip to adopt her. "What appealed to me was the look on her face." Mabel's description noted that she was good with cats, an important fact because Beth had recently adopted one.

Pet therapy wasn't on Beth's mind when she brought the frisky four- or five-month-old pup home, but her veterinarian, Dr. John North, pointed out that the dog's temperament would make her an ideal candidate. His prediction proved true. The dog found a true calling.

The hospital program was rigorous. Before each visit, Mabel had to have a bath and have her teeth and nails cleaned. Beth had to make sure both of them were in good health, and of course, Mabel's shots had to be up to date. The work reshaped their lives.

But Mabel's therapy work at the nursing home and hospital didn't change Beth's life nearly as much as what happened after the World Trade Center tragedy.

"Right after 9/11, the woman in charge of Dogs in Service called me and said they needed some people to go up to Liberty State Park to the Family Assistance Center," Beth recalls.

Beth was in sales and often took Mabel with her when she called on customers. That day, after she finished her work, she and Mabel went to the Center. It was located across the Hudson River from Ground Zero and served as a staging area for taking boatloads of New Jersey families who had lost someone in the tragedy to visit the site. The smell of the burning remains of the trade center permeated the air and smoke hung over the landscape.

She and Mabel began going to the center every day, and doing so became paramount in Beth's life. "My sales job really didn't matter to me anymore."

The Salvation Army and Red Cross volunteers noticed that some of the adults were not talking about the tragedy and suggested that maybe if Beth and Mabel just walked around that would get them started. Beth turned Mabel loose in her Dogs in Service vest. She herself would sit down while Mabel patrolled the room.

"She seemed to know which people needed to talk," Beth says. "She would go and put her head on someone's lap, and the person would start opening up to her. 'Oh, you are so cute,' one woman said. 'You know, my daughter would have loved you'—a daughter who had died in the building."

The center had an area set up for the children, and Beth asked to take Mabel there. "Some of the kids wouldn't talk to the Crisis Management people, but they would talk to Mabel. She was an angel. There was one family there that had lost its mother, and the father was there with the five kids. He had to go off with another group, and Mabel kept the kids busy, doing her tricks."

A board was set up where children could write messages to their family members who had died. The children trusted Beth and Mabel, and would ask Beth to help them.

"They would say, 'I want to write something to my daddy,'" Beth relates. "I would try to get them to wait for their mom to come back, but they would say, 'I want to write it *right now*.' So I would go with them to the board."

Mabel and Beth went back each day until January when the center was closed. The experience had truly changed Mabel. She had developed a new sensitivity. When they visited the hospital after that, she went directly to children who had terminal illnesses. "She picked them out and would go over and put her head on their laps," Beth says. "It was as if she was saying, 'This is the kid I need to work with.' To see it was amazing."

Beth changed, too. Many children at the Family Assistance Center had asked her where she taught. She would reply that she wasn't a teacher, which was literally true. "That's what I went to school for," she explains, "but I had never taught. Maybe twenty-five kids said something like that to me." Their questions and helping the children convinced her to turn her back on her sales career.

Today Beth teaches high school and coaches basketball and field hockey. "I am in heaven," she says. "I wouldn't have ever done this without Mabel because I would have never been at the Family Assistance Center without her. She's one of the best things that has ever happened to me."

The Wisdom of a Sage

Sharon Jarvis of Toronto, Ontario, worried about her elderly father. Diabetes had robbed him of his health, and though he lived with her so she could assist him, her work kept her away from the house for long hours. She had hired part-time caregivers, but between the time they left and she arrived, there were hours when he was at loose ends.

Maybe a dog would help fill the care gap, she reasoned.

She logged onto Petfinder.com and didn't hesitate about what breed to enter into the search box: she loved Shetland sheepdogs—shelties. She'd had one years before, and she knew they could be quite affectionate and loyal to their owners.

Take Me Home, an all-volunteer animal placement group based in Mississauga, Ontario, regularly checked shelters in a wide area for adoptable dogs that might otherwise be euthanized. They posted them on Petfinder.com. A volunteer had just listed an approximately eight-month-old male sheltie named *Tilou*,

French for "little wolf," who was in a shelter in Quebec. Just looking at the dog's image made Sharon think he was the answer to her prayers. She sent an e-mail to the address listed under Tilou's photo. The volunteer who replied said if the dog was still at the shelter, Take Me Home would truck him in for their next adoption day, where Sharon could meet him.

No one had adopted the dog, so he joined nineteen others that were trucked overnight from Quebec to Toronto.

"I didn't recognize him as a sheltie," Sharon said of their meeting. No one knew what his early life had been like, but his former owners had not cherished him or he wouldn't have been in the shelter in the first place. Part of his tail was missing, and his feet showed signs of a former frostbite. He was poorly groomed and scared.

"I took him outside to get better acquainted," Sharon says, "and all he wanted to do was get back in." He wasn't what she had expected, but she put her reservations aside and adopted him.

The sheltie, who looked very much like a fox, got along well with her father, which was crucial if he was to be a companion to him. In general, however, men frightened the dog, whom Sharon renamed *Sage*. To overcome his fear, Sharon handed her brothers bits of chicken to offer the dog when he came near. Sage was easy. A few tasty morsels won his heart, and "Now he thinks men are wonderful," she says with a laugh.

He settled into his new role as companion and friend, and Sharon watched his confidence grow. "He never barked at first, but now he does," Sharon says. "When I come in, it's like, 'Hello, I'm here. Hello, hello, hello.'"

One evening, Sharon was in the kitchen preparing dinner when Sage began whining and pacing back and forth between rooms.

"What's the matter with you?" Sharon asked.

He continued to whine, then turned and went out of the room. Moments later he was back, still whining and pacing.

"He wouldn't quit," Sharon said, so she stopped what she was doing and followed him. When she looked in on her father, she discovered that his blood sugar had dropped precipitously, and he had become disoriented and glassy-eyed.

"Sage was trying to tell me," Sharon recalls. She quickly gave her father something to eat, and he became himself again.

Another incident again proved Sage's sensitivity. One morning about 5:00 A.M., Sage came into Sharon's bedroom and started jumping on and off the bed.

"I tried to make him lie down beside me," she says. She resisted opening her eyes. "I'd grab his collar and try petting him because I didn't want to get up at five o'clock. 'Will you settle down?' I asked. But he wouldn't stop."

By then she was wide awake, so with a sigh, she got out of bed. Sage urged her down the hall, and as she approached her father's room, she could hear the old man moaning. Once again, he was experiencing hypoglycemia.

"Sage proved to be extremely sensitive," says Sharon. "I have another sheltie named Shelby, and she doesn't have his sensitivity at all."

Eventually, Sharon's father moved to a nursing home, and she and the dogs visit regularly. "Sage is very happy to visit. He jumps right up on the bed next to my father and lies down with him."

The two dogs are a hit with the rest of the residents as well. They shake hands and perform a repertoire of tricks Sharon has taught them.

"Dance," she commands and the two dogs rise up on their hind legs, lean against once another and move about. Then Sage bows and Shelby curtsies.

Sage's energy lets him shine in agility classes. "He gets up to the top of the A-frame and wants to play," Sharon says, so different from when she first adopted him, when he was just a frightened pup.

"He has come such a long way," she says. "He's my special boy."

A Friend Indeed

An animal control officer in Jeffersonville, Indiana, found the reddish-brown mutt with floppy ears in an alley, nursing a litter of new pups. The folks at the shelter guessed that the cute little pooch was a beagle/Pekingese mix. They named her Roofie-Toothie, alluding to the mutt's underbite, a feature that captured everyone's hearts—that, and that wagging tail of hers. The name evolved to simply "Ruthie."

Her puppies were weaned and adopted, but no one stepped forward to adopt Ruthie. Fortunately for her, everyone at the shelter loved her so much that they kept her off death row, even though the shelter was crowded.

Eventually, the shelter staff had to make room for other dogs, so they called My Southern Indiana Rescue, who placed her in a foster home. The rescue discovered that she had heartworms, so her new foster family saw her through the treatment ordeal. Once they had nursed her back to health, they posted her story on Petfinder.com, and at long last, someone inquired about Ruthie and adopted her.

Though Ruthie had gotten along with the huskies in her foster home, the adopter's Chihuahua resented her presence, and Ruthie spent her whole time in her new home under the bed. That just wouldn't do, so the adopter returned her to foster care. Poor Ruthie. Things just didn't seem to go her way.

Jonna Asher, who lived in Shelbyville, Indiana, was unaware of all of this. She and her sister, Kristi Asher, had simply decided their parents needed a dog. "We thought maybe a dog would take their mind off their troubles," Jonna says, referring to her parents' health concerns.

Myrna, Jonna's mother, liked the idea of getting a pet. She'd been around dogs growing up, and the Ashers had always had family dogs when the girls were growing up.

Jonna logged onto Petfinder.com and searched for several weeks until she came across Ruthie's photo and description. When she saw the underbite, her search stopped. She knew this was the dog. In fact, when she later heard that the dog had previously been adopted and brought back, she called it *destiny* because her maternal grandmother had owned a Pekingese with an underbite. This pooch looked like one of the family.

She told her sister that Ruthie was the dog. "She thought I was crazy because I was *so* sure."

After talking to the foster "mom," Jonna and her parents headed for Jeffersonville, which is right across the river from Louisville, so close that Jonna says Ruthie barks with a Kentucky accent.

"When we met her, she was all we could have hoped for," says Jonna. "She was an amazingly sweet, calm dog. She won our hearts immediately." When they took her for a trial walk, she didn't even pull on the leash. This was important to Jonna because her parents were in their late seventies, and her own dog, a Nova Scotia duck tolling retriever, was much too strong for them.

After four or five months in limbo, Ruthie went home with her new family and met Jonna's dog and cats.

"She gets along fine with them," says Jonna. The two dogs soon learned they had a common interest: chasing rabbits. Ruthie also had a knack for detecting moles in the yard, though Myrna says when Ruthie came up with a mouthful of dirt on one mole-digging expedition, that about cured her.

Right away, Ruthie went on her second big adventure to Metamora, a tiny canal town in southeastern Indiana where Myrna and her husband, Chris, run a gift shop. The Ashers had an apartment in back and spent part of each week there.

Ruthie soon became a great ambassador for the shop. "Everyone wanted to know if they could pet her," Myrna says.

Myrna is confined to a wheelchair, so Chris takes Ruthie out for walks around the small town. They walk by the canal to the post office, sometimes accompanied by Bear, a dog from the other side of the canal who Myrna says is king of the town. That makes Ruthie, if not the queen, the princess. She is something of a celebrity in town.

"My dad didn't want a dog at first," Jonna explains, "but he wanted to get one if Mom wanted one. Now they're best buddies."

Ruthie turned out to be more than just a buddy for Chris, who was diabetic. She's an incentive for him to stay active.

"He told me if it weren't for Ruthie, he wouldn't go for a walk every day. And he needs exercise," Myrna says gratefully.

Ruthie has also turned out to be a medical alert dog.

One night Myrna awoke with a start to find Ruthie licking Chris's face. She tried to get Chris to respond, but he couldn't—he was having a seizure. Once the dog saw that Myrna was awake, Ruthie raced out of the room to alert Jonna, who came running. Myrna called 911, and then the two women restrained Chris to keep him from inadvertently hurting himself until help arrived. The episode was a result of a precipitous drop in his blood sugar.

"We didn't know Ruthie had medical training," Jonna says wryly.

When Chris spent a week in the hospital, Ruthie paced through the house, looking for him. "She even cried," Kristi recalls.

Of course, Ruthie's not perfect. "She snores loud enough to bring down the rafters," Jonna says with a laugh, "and she has 'the claw.' If you're petting her and you stop, out comes the claw. They warned us about it at the shelter." Ruthie uses the claw to knock the newspaper down when Chris is reading it—anything to get his attention.

Hunter, business ambassador, medical assistant, princess—she is all of these. Says Myrna, "She doesn't know she's a dog!"

"I can't even express how much Ruthie has touched us," Jonna says. "I can't imagine where we would be without her."

A Helping Paw

The veterinarian thought she had seen it all, but the tiny black puppy's condition sickened her. Someone had kicked the little dog so hard his jaw was fractured—broken in half. His mouth hung open, and he cowered from her touch. The little fellow was hardly even weaning age—about five weeks old.

Seeing such abuse was enough to make her lose her faith in humans.

After repairing the jaw, the vet called her friend, Gina McCaughran, and filled her in. Would Gina take the little pooch, nurse him back to health, and then find him a permanent home?

The answer was, of course, *yes*. Gina is the director of S.A.F.E. Dog Rescue, a group that she founded in Sultan, Washington.

Gina and her then seven-year-old daughter, Gabrielle, embarked on a mission to help the little guy. They named him St. Nick because it was the holiday season, although he was far from jolly.

"He screamed whenever anyone came in the room," Gina recalls sadly, "and he would run and hide. He was just terrified of people."

The jaw would take time to heal, and he couldn't eat, so Gina put together a liquid concoction, and she and Gabrielle fed it to him with a syringe—every four hours like clockwork—night and day—for the first month.

He overcame his fear of the two of them, and he loved their dogs. But he was still afraid of other people.

"Our next job was to get him socialized," Gina explains. "We knew we couldn't keep him; our whole point is to find dogs other homes. So we just took him everywhere we went."

By three months, his jaw had healed and he was coming around with people, so Gina posted him on Petfinder.com.

His photo showed an irresistible black fuzzball of a puppy. But his description undoubtedly elicited most of the inquiries.

"His was a sad story, and we get a lot of responses to sad stories," Gina says. "We went through the applications and interviewed people, and we turned down a lot. Obviously he needed a special home."

That special home belonged to Lindsey McClincy of Mukilteo, Washington. She was looking for a chocolate Labrador retriever puppy. Nick's photo came up as a lab mix, and once she saw his photo, that was close enough.

What made Lindsey's application stand out was all that she herself had been through. She was diagnosed with Crohn's disease when she was twenty-one, which led to a liver disease. The steroids used to treat it led to avascular necrosis in both of her hips. For several years, she depended upon a cane or crutches, or even a wheelchair at times, to get around.

"She needed the unconditional love and companionship of a dog," says Gina, "and her application was wonderful."

Gina did a home visit, and her only reservation was the future. Her job was to look out for the welfare of the dog, so she asked the hard question: What would happen to Nick if something happened to Lindsey?

"Lindsey assured me that her mom, who had a dog, would care for Nick if anything happened to her," Gina says. That was enough for Gina. She approved the placement.

Lindsey and Nick bonded right away. He settled in and began to grow—and grow.

"He's huge!" Lindsey says. "He's not a chocolate Lab; he's more like a black Lab/Great Dane mix, and he thinks he's a lap dog. You say, 'Come sit,' and you expect him to sit on the floor, but he comes right up and moves you over and sits himself right down on the couch next to you."

Nick's affectionate nature is not limited to his owner. Lindsey works with a feral cat group, taking in cats that are pregnant. Once the babies are born and weaned, she has the mothers spayed and then releases them. She was astonished at Nick's behavior toward one litter of kittens.

"From the day those babies were born, he treated them as if they were his," Lindsey says. "He would just go over and nudge them and keep them from going where they weren't supposed to go."

The nurturing behavior extended to her six-month-old niece. "She was starting to crawl," Lindsey relates, "and Nick knew she wasn't supposed to go in certain areas. He would gently lean down with his face in front of her to block the way. He's a gentle giant."

Hip replacement surgery loomed for Lindsey, and she knew she needed help. She training Nick to be her assistance dog. She didn't enroll him in a formal training program, instead she went online and did research on training.

"I taught him to open doors for me and to pick things up when I drop them," she explains. "He was so easily trainable that it only took about three times with each command. I put a little fixture on the doorknobs, and I told him to grab it and pull. It unlocked the door, and then I told him to push. If I dropped something, I just told him to bring it."

After her third surgery, Lindsey couldn't bend over to take off her socks. Nick did it for her. "I just shook my foot and said, 'Take it.' He gently nibbled it, and pulled back and back. I didn't even feel it, and he absolutely was so proud of himself when he helped me. He just loved to please me."

Lindsey recovered from her hip surgeries, but Nick still loves to help. "I don't even have to give him a command; I just wait at the door, and he opens it. Anyone that comes over to the house—he loves to take off their socks."

During her surgeries and recovery, Lindsey moved in with her parents, and their dog Gracie, a husky/shepherd mix, wasn't so sure she wanted another dog in her domain.

"Gracie definitely ruled the roost, and it was hard for her to adjust," Lindsey explains. But Nick's charismatic personality won her over. It was as if he said, 'You're going to like me and that's that.'"

Gracie relented and the two of them lived in the same house in happy harmony.

Coming from the background he did, Nick's attitude is just short of miraculous, thanks to some wonderful people. And Nick? He deserves his name: Saint Nick.

Out of Stir

Digger came to the Muhlenberg County Humane Society in Greenville, Kentucky, after he was seized in an animal cruelty case. The six-month-old Great Dane was half the size he should have been because his owners hadn't fed him properly.

In addition, Digger had been physically abused, leaving him skittish. The staff thought it unlikely he would be adopted because he didn't put his best paw forward when potential adopters came to the shelter. No doubt about it: Digger needed help.

Fortunately, the humane society had just the plan for him—the Death Row Dog Program, where personal attention and training would help him overcome his rocky start in life. Every eight to ten weeks, fifteen dogs whose behavior needed tweaking went to live at the Green River Correctional Complex, where inmates reshaped them to increase their adoptability. Inmates lined up to be part of the program, and only thirty got to participate. They were paired up to take care of the fifteen dogs.

Kim Pennington, director of the humane society, launched the program. "It was my dream, but there were a lot of people behind it pushing to make it happen," she explains. The program was the first of its kind in Kentucky.

Digger was turned over to two handlers, cellmates at the medium-security facility.

The handlers teach the dogs commands like *sit, stay, down,* and *come,* and how to walk on a loose leash. The dogs live with the inmates in their cells, and they exercise them in a training area that has toys and a small swimming pool for the dogs.

The inmates are with the dogs all day, so they take them out regularly to relieve themselves. Anticipating, however, that the dogs' adopters might be away from home during the day, the handlers also housetrain the dogs.

Twice a week, the inmates meet with Kim, who as the master trainer gives them instructions. The rest of the time, she says, "they fly solo."

Digger gained confidence under the care of his handlers, and the inmates came to care deeply for him.

"The inmates are sad when they have to give up a dog," Kim relates. "Those who have been in prison for a long time have often buried their emotions. The dog program teaches them that they still do have a heart; that they can still hurt. It kind of keeps them human."

Besides training the dogs, Kim notices, the program helps the prisoners relate to their families more positively. "Once someone is incarcerated, their families don't want much to do with them," she explains. "The visits are difficult because what do you talk about? It's not like the inmate can say, 'Today I went to the mall.' But they *can* talk about their dogs. The families visit in a big room, and the dogs get to come, too. The dogs are a good icebreaker—and they also get exposed to children that way," another plus on the adoptability scale.

Graduation Day arrived for Digger. He had served his time at Green River, but would fate relegate him to a kennel at the humane society? Would anyone want the once-neglected pooch who had been rehabilitated in prison? The staff posted him on Petfinder.com, and the magic of the Internet began to do its work.

Five hours away in Chattanooga, Tennessee, Beth Payne was looking on Petfinder.com for a big dog. "We'd always had small or medium-sized dogs. We already had two dogs: a rescue dog named Benny—a min pin/rat terrier mix, who we adopted from a shelter, and a beagle mix named Buddy, who my husband rescued from a dumpster outside his office."

When Beth came across Digger, his photo appealed to her, but it was his story that really touched her heart. She told her husband, Bob, and their son, Braeden, about the dog, and they agreed that he was the one for them.

The shelter approved their application, and Digger, whom they renamed Beau, came to live with the family.

Beau, thrust into a new situation, took a little while to warm up to his new humans, but he immediately loved the dogs. Buddy the beagle became his best friend. The training Beau had received at Green River made his transition into the family easier because even while he was getting used to his new home, he was well behaved. It didn't take long for him to acclimate.

"Beau is the most loving, patient, and kindest dog we have ever had," Beth says, adding, "Did I also mention the laziest? His favorite pastime is sleeping on our twin-size guest bed, which is almost too small for him." Quite a different story than when Beau was only half the size he should have been.

"I thank God for him every day," Beth says. The formerly abused and unloved Great Dane has become a "large" part of the Payne Family.

It's a Miracle

Years ago, a little girl's heart was about to break when a mean boy in her neighborhood abused his Boston terrier. One night the little girl slipped out of her house and took the dog from the boy's backyard. She walked the dog down the street to the house of a friendly old woman whose own dog had recently died, fibbing that the terrier was a stray and needed a home. The woman took the dog in, and he lived a happy life with his new owner.

The gutsy little girl was Arlene Lavoie of Manchester, Connecticut. "I'm still a sucker for a mistreated animal," she says. "If I see a dog left in a car, I call the police. I call so often, they know my name."

With her lifelong concern for pets, it was no wonder Arlene responded to the story of a little tan Chihuahua that needed a home.

"This little dog had been thrown away in a garbage bin in the Bronx," says Arlene. The dog was in a sorry state and her rescuer rushed her to a veterinarian, who removed a large cancerous tumor on her stomach. He had to remove her teeth and part of her lower jaw when he found another tumor there. The dog ended up in the intensive care unit. She only weighed two pounds, and the vet said it would be a miracle if she survived.

Arlene Lavoie, of course, knew nothing of this yet. She was home in Manchester, learning to mouse around on the new computer her daughter had given her. She happened to stumble onto Petfinder.com—*just looking*. Arlene didn't plan to ever get another dog because her heart was still recovering from the loss of her poodle, Lady. Besides, she still had her little Rowdy, a Chihuahua whom she had rescued some years earlier.

But when Arlene read the rescued dog's story, she knew the odds of her being adopted weren't great. Arlene figured the dog's medical issues would dissuade adopters—and she was right. She later learned that one potential adopter had expressed interest, but then had backed off when they found the dog would need special care. The dog's age, too, would work against her. At twelve years old, she was no longer a bouncy little pup. That didn't bother Arlene one bit. In fact, she saw it as something of an advantage.

"My husband and I used to volunteer at the Connecticut Humane Society and I saw these little dogs who were surrendered because their owners had died," she says. It made perfect sense to Arlene for a senior citizen to adopt a senior dog. If she got a puppy, it might outlive her and be left behind.

When Arlene's application was approved by the rescue group, the founder of the group drove to Manchester with the precious little bundle. She left a kennel for the dog, whom Arlene promptly named Miracle.

"I don't go for caging animals," Arlene explains, "but I thought this was what she was used to. She *howled*. I took her out of the cage and put her in bed with me. She had gone through so many changes; all she did was whimper through the night. It broke my heart. By the next morning, both of us were so darned tired from being up so late that I picked her up and put her on my chest and she just cuddled up there, and we both fell asleep on the couch."

Arlene surmised that Miracle had been a puppy mill dog who was no longer wanted when she developed health problems. The muscles in her legs were undeveloped.

"When she walked," Arlene recalls sadly, "she would fall over." Her new "mom" began taking her on very short walks to strengthen those muscles. It took time, but gradually the exercise paid off and the pooch developed strong legs. Besides the physical therapy, Arlene had to mound Miracle's food into a peak so the dog could get it into her mouth. Not everyone would have been willing to take the time needed to nurture Miracle, but it's part of Arlene's giving nature.

Arlene worried about how the tiny dog would tolerate Connecticut winters, so she ordered a pair of dog boots and little coat and sweater. Arlene's husband, Babe, had the idea of cutting the cuffs off a pair of gloves and putting them on Miracle's perky ears to protect them from the cold. All bundled up, she looks like a little Eskimo. Armed with her winter get-up, Miracle can go out to the little pop-up tent the couple set up for her to keep one area of the yard free of snow.

Six months after Miracle arrived, Rowdy passed away at thirteen.

Arlene is not planning to adopt another dog, but then again, she wasn't planning to adopt Miracle—and she is still "just looking" on Petfinder.com. The best advice for this guardian angel? Never say never.

Every Wish Way But Loose

Sojo was a worry to Bonnie Amsden, the animal control officer for the City of Pevely, Missouri. A family had brought the Jack Russell terrier home with them from out of state, but he kept getting loose every time the kids opened the door. Bonnie would pick up Sojo, return him, and remind the family that they had to keep him on their property. It was the law. Finally, the mother of the house brought Sojo to the shelter and asked Bonnie if she could find him a home.

"Sure, I'll give it a try," Bonnie replied.

She posted Sojo on Petfinder.com and waited. Bonnie didn't wait long because at six months old, with wiry hair and whiskers, Sojo was an adorable little dog.

"The people that first adopted him had a fence," Bonnie explains. "That was a requirement. But he was just a wild fellow and could climb fences. He loved to run."

Back Sojo came to the shelter.

A man adopted him the second time—his third home. Bonnie explained that Sojo had a tendency to get out, but that did not dissuade the man. "He had Sojo three days and brought him back," recalls Bonnie.

Bonnie was beginning to get nervous about Sojo's fate.

Then Sandra and Arthur McCoy, who live on an acreage outside of DeSoto, Missouri, entered Sojo's life. Their silky terrier had passed away, and both Sandra and her other dog, Tizzette, a cairn terrier, were missing her keenly.

"I take care of my elderly mother," Sandra says, "so I am homebound and my dogs are my company and entertainment. I found Petfinder.com and began looking at pets listed at local shelters. I told myself I was just looking." While "just looking," she happened upon Sojo's photo on the Pevely shelter's pet list. "He was so cute, but the eyes—they were that of a tired soul," recalls Sandra. A few days later, she noticed his photo was gone and he was in the happy "tails" section of the Pevely site.

"That's good," she thought, relieved.

"A couple of weeks later, I was back on Petfinder.com, and there was his picture again," Sandra reports. She was curious and called the Pevely shelter.

Bonnie explained Sojo's adoption failures and told Sandra how dire the situation was becoming. The pup had once been potty trained, she said, but not anymore. He had once played nicely with other dogs; now it was a gamble whether he was going to play nicely or get snippy. He was confused, that was apparent, and shelter life was taking its toll on poor Sojo.

After explaining all of this, Bonnie asked Sandra if she wanted to meet him.

"I'm on my way," Sandra replied.

The pup had an immediate affinity for Sandra, perhaps something to do with the bacon she had stuffed in her pocket before leaving home. He sniffed her pocket, and then sat down in front of her, minding his manners. "*Smart dog,*" Sandra thought, and signed the papers to adopt him. She put him in a carrier and off they went.

When Sandra brought him into the house, Tizzette looked at the carrier as if to say, "*Whatcha got in there?*"

"I opened it up, and they were happy to see each other," Sandra recalls. Sojo was home, and Tizzette had a companion again.

Arthur McCoy renamed the dog *Wishbone*, after the dog in the television series. The couple quickly discovered that the energetic terrier could open doors and chew off leashes. He also proved to be quite a digger.

Wishbone was easy to train, and Sandra's grandson, Jadyn set out to teach him tricks. The terrier learned to shake hands, put his paws together as if praying, and lie down and play dead when someone says, "*Bang!*"

"Anything we think of, he can do," Sandra says proudly.

Wishbone keeps them entertained. One hot day when the McCoys were having a picnic in the backyard, Sandra, who was inside, heard her guests laughing. She hurried out to see what was going on. There was Wishbone, sitting in the birdbath, getting cool.

Sandra knew Wishbone was clever from the moment she met him, and his antics keep her from becoming depressed about her mother's deteriorating health. The elderly woman has Alzheimer's disease and has begun to have weak spells that sometimes end in seizures. Sandra has learned that there is more to the little dog than fun and games.

She had trained Wishbone to stay in uncarpeted areas because he wasn't completely dependable about his housetraining at first, and he was very obedient about staying put. One day when he was in the kitchen, Sandra walked her mother to the bathroom door, and then let the older woman go into the bathroom alone.

"I was nearby and kept checking on her," Sandra relates. "'I'm fine, I'm fine. I'll be out in just a minute,' she would tell me. I sat down at my computer to wait, and I could hear my mother moving around. Then Wish came flying into the room, jumping at the bathroom door. I knew something was wrong because he had left the kitchen and come clear through the living room, across the carpet. I jumped up and went over to the bathroom. When I got the door open, my mother was sitting there with her head down between her knees, and she was grasping the sink. She was having a weak spell, and Wishbone had alerted me."

Another time, Sandra put a skillet on the range to melt some butter and got distracted helping her mother at the other end of the house.

"Wish kept running in," Sandra recalls, "and I kept saying, 'Get back in that kitchen.' Then I remembered I was cooking. He was warning me."

With the exception of Sandra's mother, Wishbone usually was too busy to focus on any one person, so when Sandra noticed him fussing around and jumping on one of her son's friends, she was suspicious. She asked the young man if Wishbone had always behaved this way around him.

"Pretty much," the friend replied.

Sandra knew immediately that something was physically wrong with the young man and Wishbone was sensitive to it in the same way he was sensitive to her mother's spells. She asked the visitor about it.

The young man looked at her with a shocked expression. "I have Parkinson's disease." He'd known for six months, which coincided with Wishbone's adoption and probably accounted for the dog's excessive attentiveness when the young man visited the McCoys.

Wishbone, true to his breed, is a handful. He can jump fences and loves to run wild, and it takes constant watchfulness to keep him safe. Fortunately, he has a home in the country where the dangers are few, and the little dog has found a family who loves him unconditionally. The McCoys recognize what an outstanding little fellow Wishbone is.

The Detect-o Dog

Although it may not occur as often, purebred dogs do indeed end up in shelters, just as mixed breeds do. Sugar Bear is a case in point. Her first owner purchased her from a breeder, but when the young woman went off to college, she relinquished the German shepherd to The Animal Humane Society in Golden Valley, Minnesota.

It wasn't long before Sugar Bear was adopted again, this time by the children of an elderly couple who felt their parents needed the companionship of a dog. All went well until one of the parents became terminally ill. It was back to the shelter for Sugar Bear.

Her next family proclaimed she was too much responsibility, and another couple confined the one-and-a-half-year-old dog in their laundry room for three days when they found her to be too exuberant.

After four homes, Sugar Bear's future was looking grim, and her purebred status almost caused her to miss her next big chance.

Julie Olson of Coon Rapids, Minnesota, had just moved into a townhouse that allowed pets. Before she had even unpacked, she began browsing on Petfinder.com.

"I was looking for a German shepherd/husky mix," explains Julie, "because I like the traits of both breeds."

She saw Sugar Bear's listing on the site and decided to go have a look at her.

"I spent some time with her at the shelter," Julie says, "but she was a purebred and I thought she would have an easy time finding a home."

So Julie left The Animal Humane Society to visit other mixed breed pets she'd seen listed on Petfinder.com. "One dog I really liked was adopted right out from under me by people who identified her first. I was happy for them, but disappointed for me."

Julie returned home and began unpacking. "Something told me to go back to The Animal Humane Society."

When she arrived, Sugar Bear was still there. "I went to the front and said, 'I think I'm in love with Sugar Bear. May I take her out of her kennel?'"

The two of them went to an adoption room to get better acquainted. The time spent with Sugar Bear convinced Julie she wanted to adopt the dog.

"I kept telling her I would be taking her home with me," Julie recalls. "But it was late, and the staff didn't have time to finish the adoption, so I had to leave her." Julie felt bad about it, but the staff put a card on Sugar Bear's kennel saying her adoption was pending. The shelter was closed the following day, a Monday, but

Julie arranged to take off work the rest of the week. On Tuesday, she finalized the adoption, and she and Sugar Bear, whom she renamed Tikaani, a native American word for *wolf*, went home to get acquainted.

Julie's intention was to put Tikaani in a crate when she wasn't home. But every time Julie would return home, the dog would be out. "I reinforced it with zip ties, but when I came back, she was out and the door was still closed," Julie says, mystified. "I asked her, 'Did you teleport yourself? Did you call Scotty?' I'd read about dogs partially escaping and strangling themselves, which terrified me, so I just started leaving her out of her kennel. I just limited what she had access to."

For the most part, that worked, although one time Tikanni entertained herself by stringing out toilet paper, and the dowel that held it came off. Tikanni hid it. When Julie arrived home, it was obvious that Tikaani had been up to no good. "She sat at the top of the stairs with her ears tucked, but she wouldn't go any farther," Julie recalls.

Another time, Tikanni pulled all of Julie's winter clothes out of the closet to eat the treats Julie had inadvertently left in the pockets. Julie could hardly be angry, for what resourceful dog would miss an opportunity like that?

Tikaani had adjusted quickly to her new home, sleeping through the night from the very first. Then one night, two weeks after her arrival, the dog deviated from her normal pattern. "She kept me awake all night, begging to go out. She continually came and nudged me. She didn't seem too distressed, and I told her to go away." To Julie, it was mainly annoying. "I'd fall asleep, and she would wake me, look me in the eye with her ears pricked forward. Once she got my attention, she would relax."

Tikaani didn't succeed in getting Julie up, and it was only the next morning that she realized that something was wrong. "I got my coffee and turned on the news and noticed it was pretty cold in the house, even though I had on this big fuzzy robe. The furnace wasn't kicking on." She fiddled with the thermostat, but nothing happened. "That kind of freaked me out, so I turned it off completely and opened the door."

For Julie, the whole thing was like a déjà vu. When she was a child, a stray dog had adopted her family. One night the dog, Tina, had kept insisting upon going out all night. "The difference was that my mom didn't ignore her," explains Julie. "She kept letting her in and out. Tina made my mom keep the door open." The next morning, the family discovered the furnace was malfunctioning and carbon monoxide was leaking into the air.

Now, years later, Tikaani had tried to warn her new guardian in a similar way. Later in the day, Julie learned the furnace had a broken switch that kept it from coming on, and there was not a carbon monoxide problem.

"But Tikaani knew something was wrong because she hasn't acted that way since," Julie says. "I'm never going to ignore her again, and I'll never be without a dog. I have absolute confidence that if anything happens that I need to know about, she'll alert me. Dogs know some things we don't."

Love at First Byte

At first glance, the passersby had a hard time distinguishing what it was they were seeing. Perhaps it was a rabbit, the way it was hopping around. When they pulled over, their curiosity quickly turned to horror. It was a small white-and-buff-colored dog, frantically trying to extricate itself from a shroud of chicken wire around its lower body.

The people rushed to the female cockapoo's aid and were sickened to realize that the dog's entrapment, by the looks of it, had been intentional: Someone had wrapped the dog up and abandoned her. The good Samaritans removed the wire, took her to their home, and called the Animal Rescue League (ARL) of El Paso. The next morning, the foundling, who was about two years old, delivered a litter of eight puppies.

Once the mama dog's pups were weaned, the ARL staff listed her on Petfinder.com and began taking her to adoption days to find a lifelong home for her. At one of these events, she was adopted, but the people returned her the very same day, saying that she had jumped over their six-foot fence. Once again, the shelter listed her on Petfinder.com.

In Oshkosh, Wisconsin, the Sorensen family saw the cockapoo, listed as Bunny, on the site. They very much wanted to adopt a dog after losing their beloved Tabitha, herself a rescue dog, and when they read Bunny's heart-wrenching story, it was love at first byte. They didn't even need to see her photo, which hadn't been posted yet, to know they wanted her.

Several evenings later when ARL added her photo, Ryan Sorensen, then nine, called his mom, who was playing bingo.

"Mom, you have to see this picture," he said. "Bunny looks just like Tabitha."

When Debbie arrived home, Ryan was waiting with more entreaties. "We have to call, Mom," he insisted.

It was too late to call the shelter, but to placate her son, Debbie immediately sent an e-mail.

The next morning, Ryan popped out of bed, once again urging his mom to call.

Debbie did so and learned that Bunny was still there, and she set things in motion to adopt the dog, furnishing references, including the name and number of their veterinarian.

"Our vet knows that dogs are definitely family with us," says Debbie, "so I knew he would give us a good reference."

While the Sorensens waited for ARL to approve their application, Bunny was headed for an adoption day. "We were a nervous wreck," Debbie recalls. "We were praying no one would adopt her."

Their prayers were answered. Even though small dogs are in high demand, no one chose Bunny that day. A few days later, the shelter approved the Sorensens' application.

The next challenge was getting her to Wisconsin. The family had already been checking with airlines. They found one that had an air-conditioned cargo hold but wouldn't fly a live animal if the outside temperature reached a certain point, and this was July. El Paso was heating up, and the Sorensens were sweating it out in Oshkosh.

"We were so concerned about the stress and fear involved for her to fly alone in a cargo area that my husband considered flying to El Paso and then renting a car to drive her back," Debbie says. "Were we bitten by her cuteness or what?"

But everything fell into place, and on July 7, the temperature cooperated. ARL staffer Jeannette Velasquez took Bunny to the airport, and the dog set out on her journey.

The Sorensons drove to the airport in Green Bay, Wisconsin, to await Bunny's homecoming.

"The airline counter person was so taken by our Bunny story that she told us about an area outside the terminal where we could stand and watch and take pictures of Bunny being deplaned," Debbie relates. "It was very touching to see the little crate carrying this poor soul being so gently lifted out of the plane and moving down the conveyor belt."

The crate was loaded onto the baggage cart, and the family hurried inside to claim her.

They had worried about the emotional trauma of flying, but when the ties binding her crate were cut and the cage door opened, their fears went unrealized.

Out bounded the little dog, her huge tail wagging as fast as it would go. "She kissed everyone," Debbie remembers, "including the airline counter attendant."

Ryan led her outside, and she tried to greet every person they passed as if to say, "I'm here, I'm here. I'm finally here."

Bunny, renamed Summer, curled up next to Ryan on the drive home. "It was as if she just knew this was where she was destined to find happiness and love," Debbie said. "I will never understand how some people can do the horrible things they do to defenseless animals such as Summer. Nor do I understand how this dog can give us humans another chance to prove we're not like those people that hurt her."

But Summer's loving disposition makes the Sorensens believe that she indeed can forgive and forget.

Family Relations

Until his retirement in the late 1940s, John Murphy was a firefighter with Ladder Company 29 in the Bronx. One day, a stray dog wandered by the station. Lt. Murphy took him in, named him Kerry after the county from which the Irishman had immigrated, and the dog's role as a firehouse dog was sealed.

One day an alarm came in, and the crew jumped onto the ladder truck. Off they went, Kerry riding in the cab. When they arrived on the scene, Kerry must have heard something because he went dashing down some stairs and found a mother dog and three puppies in the basement of the building. He carried two puppies to safety. When he returned, the mother dog had collapsed while attempting to rescue the third puppy. A firefighter came to Kerry's assistance, and the dogs were all rescued.

The story made the newspapers, and Kerry was a hero. He continued working at the firehouse for about nine years and lost his life in the line of duty, according to the preface of a children's book, *Kerry, the Fire-Engine Dog,* published in 1949. Upon his death, the firefighters buried him in the Canine and Animal Cemetery in Westchester County, New York.

About fifty years later, the Rodinos of South Orange, New Jersey, were looking for a dog to adopt.

"We had been looking for about a year," says Carol Rodino. "We had just about given up finding a small, mixed breed, non-shedding puppy that needed a home."

She logged onto Petfinder.com one last time before buying a dog. "Up popped two Shih Tzu/poodle puppies, a male and female, in a town I'd never heard of, about twenty-four miles away." The place was Lakeland Animal Haven in Kenvil, New Jersey. "There were no pictures of the dogs, but I knew that they would go fast, so I jumped in my car and raced out there."

Carol told Barbara Martin, the manager at Lakeland, that the male pup was just what she was looking for, but that he seemed to be barking a lot.

Barbara assured Carol that he was beside himself from being in the shelter, that he would be fine when she got him by himself. It didn't even take that: When Carol picked him up and held him, he quieted down immediately.

By then, it was nine o'clock. Barbara asked Carol if she wanted to take the dog home.

"How can I take him home?" she asked. "I don't have a bed or anything for him. The stores are closed." She arranged to come back the following morning, and then felt guilty that she had left him for one more night in a shelter.

Carol still didn't want to get her family's hopes up for fear that something would go awry, so she didn't tell them about the dog. The next morning she rushed around and bought supplies, then returned to the shelter to adopt the five-month-old pup. On the way home, she stopped at the veterinarian's, then left the dog at a shop to get him groomed.

At the end of the school day, she picked up her younger boys, still not giving up her secret, and took them back with her to the groomer's.

There, on the groomer's table, sat the dog, wearing a kerchief.

"Can we take him home?" one of the boys asked.

"You can't leave him here," the groomer said.

Only then did it dawn on the boys that the dog was theirs. "We thought we were going to look at a dog and go home and discuss it," explains Chris Rodino, who was nine at the time.

The first night was a learning experience. "We didn't have any experience with puppies," recalls John, twelve at the time, "so we put him in a crate in the basement. He cried and cried. We got him, and put him in the kitchen and closed the door, and he cried and cried. That night, and for the next couple of months, he slept in my room."

He graduated to Carol's room. "When my husband is out of town, he jumps up on the bed and puts his head on the pillow like a person," she says, laughing.

The dog has a ravenous appetite. "He's a dog who loves his food," says Carol. "He's like a seagull. The food never hits the ground."

Knowing this, Carol decided to close him up in the kitchen when she served Thanksgiving dinner so he wouldn't pester her guests.

"When I went to get more turkey, I found him sitting on a bench at the kitchen table like a person, and he had eaten the whole side of the turkey carcass. What was I to do? I had seventeen people, sitting at the table. I went ahead and carved the side he couldn't reach."

One thing that comes naturally to the dog is relaxing. The Rodinos say he is something of a couch potato. "One time he hadn't been feeling well," Carol relates, "so I was trying to make him more comfortable. I bought him this little couch. I put it down with all the packaging still on it, and he jumped onto it and wouldn't get out. We had to cut the wrappings off and slide them out from under him. He knew it was his couch."

The twenty-pound bundle of dog is just what the Rodinos had hoped for. He is fiercely loyal and very affectionate. "He's such a little dog," John says, "just twenty pounds, but he thinks he can take on any dog."

"We still can't believe our good fortune at finding him," says Carol. After her long search for the perfect dog, she felt it was more than good fortune that had led her to this particular one that looked like the one in *Kerry, the Fire-Engine Dog.* She hadn't been looking for a "Kerry" necessarily, but when she saw the little black dog with the same white face and chest as the pooch in the book, she knew it was meant to be because John Murphy, the firefighter who found the stray, was Carol's grandfather.

The family named its new member *Kerry.*

One of the Family

The shoebox sitting on the doorstep at the Fort Lewis Stray Animal Facility in Tacoma, Washington, was sealed with duct tape. The person who arrived to open up the shelter picked up the box and took it inside. Scrawled on the lid were the words: *Gone to Iraq.*

Off came the tape from the airtight box and out came a whirling dervish of teeth that sank into the rescuer.

The dervish turned out to be a tiny hairless Chinese crested dog, filthy from being in its own excrement in the box. He quickly retreated to a corner of the room, snarling and growling.

The shelter person called two volunteers, Susan Pfeiffer and Pam McLaren, with Crest-Care Inc., a national Chinese crested rescue organization. Pam went to the shelter to pick up the dog.

"When we got him, he was wanting to Cujo everyone," Susan says, but she understood that he had been through a lot for his young age of three or four months. The two women gave him a warm bath, put him in a sleep sack, and he fell asleep. The little pup, now named Zephyr, had been through quite an ordeal.

He bonded with Susan, but it fell to her fifteen-year-old Chinese crested, Cinder, to help Zephyr overcome the trauma he had suffered. Cinder herself had been through bad times too. Susan had rescued her eight years earlier after children had set her on fire.

"The dogs watch what the others do," explains Susan. "Cinder did more work with Zephyr than we did. He watched her play, and he would play. He watched her eat, and he would eat. He did everything she did. She's the great healer."

Susan posted Zephyr's photo on Petfinder.com to find a permanent home for him. His photo showed a cute little dog with a hairless body, mostly dark skinned except for his chest, which was pink, peppered with gray spots. Long black hair draped from his erect ears, and his crest looked as if it might have covered his eyes had it not been tied up. His fuzzy face had a blend of colors, including a frosting of white on his muzzle. His lower legs wore "socks" of white hair, and he had a white plume of a tail.

"I was a little reluctant to post the picture because the movie *How to Lose a Guy in Ten Days* had just come out and he looked exactly like the dog in the movie. I was afraid we'd get every weirdo wanting to adopt him," Susan says.

But instead she got Marty and Terri Borden, not tempted by a Hollywood fad, but very compassionate, according to Susan.

Marty had seen a Chinese crested at a dog show and told his wife, Terri, he wanted one. Later, "she was talking to one of the women she worked with who didn't know what they looked like,"

Marty says. "They went on the Web and went to Petfinder.com. There was Zephyr."

Terri alerted Marty, who went online, too, and then e-mailed Susan, expressing interest in the dog. "I told her about the dogs we already had and that they had their own room and had health insurance." Those dogs were a Great Dane, Sybil, and a Boston terrier, Rosie.

The whole Borden pack drove to meet Zephyr at an obedience class Susan was teaching.

"I remember the meeting very well," Marty recalls. "We had a heck of a time finding the place, after dark, in the pouring rain. We took our camper van because we had Sybil and Rosie with us. Susan wanted us to bring them because I think she was a little concerned about Sybil—she was so big. Once she saw what a totally gentle creature she is, everything was fine."

The Bordens tried to make friends with Zephyr, but he was skittish. "He would just spin and spin, just out of range for us to touch him," says Marty. "We gave him treats, and finally he let us get a little closer." But Marty and Terri were still afraid that Zephyr's reluctance to warm up to them would stop Susan from letting them take Zephyr home.

He needn't have worried. Susan was impressed with the Bordens as a potential family for Zephyr, and the adoption went forward. She brought the dog over to their house to do one last home check. When it passed muster, she slipped away. Zephyr was in the backyard with Marty and the dogs, unaware that his life had just changed.

"When we came back inside, Zephyr searched all over the house for Susan," Marty recalls, "and when he couldn't find her, he actually started to cry real tears. I'd never seen that before in a dog." Zephyr settled down fairly quickly, but just to make sure he felt safe, Marty wrapped him up and held him on his chest all night like a baby.

From time to time, Zephyr has episodes of what looks like post-traumatic stress syndrome to Marty. "He'll crouch down with a look of absolute terror in his eyes. It breaks my heart."

Most of the time Zephyr is just an ordinary dog, full of vitality, who enjoys trips in the camper van to bluegrass festivals and charity dog events. He likes to bug his "sister," Rosie, biting her ears, until she gets fed up and "speaks" to him in a mean voice. He withdraws for a little while, and then starts pestering her again, like a regular little "brother." Zephyr has become one of the family.

Hank the Cow Dog To-Be

Hank, whom the shelter listed as a great Dane/mastiff mix, had a tarnished reputation. A family with miniature pinschers had adopted him and when one of the dogs snapped at Hank, he reacted. His size alone made it an uneven fight, and the min pin was injured. The family took him back to the shelter.

This black mark on the record of a black dog, notoriously harder to get adopted, kept Hank languishing in his run at Heart of Jackson Humane Society in Holton, Kansas. Would he ever find a "forever" home?

The staff was relieved one day to get a call from Keri Erickson of Gypsum, Kansas. She liked the looks of the dog she has seen on Petfinder.com and wanted to meet him. One of the things that appealed to Keri was that the photo of Hank showed him with a teenage girl. "I have kids out at the farm sometimes, so he needed to get along with children. The description said he was a nice big dog, and I thought, well, we have a nice big yard."

Keri had not owned a dog when she was growing up because her father was allergic to them. Now she was newly married, and she and her husband, Kevin, had just bought a house. It was a perfect time to adopt one. Kevin wanted a St. Bernard puppy, but "I didn't just want his dog," Keri explains. "I wanted my own dog."

A coworker of Keri's who volunteered at the local humane society suggested Keri look on Petfinder.com. Keri did. She started her search locally, but her brother lived in Topeka and she reasoned that she could check on dogs there the next time she went to visit him. She expanded her search on Petfinder to a regional one, taking in a larger area from which to choose. This search turned up Hank.

Keri headed off with a crate in her truck, certain that Hank was the dog for her.

"The shelter was out in the country," she recalls, "so to get acquainted with him, I took him out for a walk along a dirt road. He really enjoyed the walk, and I thought that would work out well because I like to go for runs, and we live out in the country."

Of course, Hank had never lived on a farm, and as she drove toward home, Keri wondered how he would react to their hog and piglets. "After all, he would *eat* pork chops."

Her worries were groundless. The former shelter dog took to life in the country from the start. He approached the pigs curiously, gave them a sniff and a good kiss.

"I think he thought they were puppies," Keri says. The Ericksons didn't have cows yet but she expected Hank to get along just as well with them when they did get them.

Hank's gentle nature continued to shine through when a five-year-old girl came to the farm for a visit. She asked to take Hank for a walk, so Keri leashed him up. Off the child and the dog went.

"He must have outweighed her by a hundred pounds," Keri says. "He could have dragged her three miles down the road." But he didn't. He was perfect, never even tugging on the leash.

Soon after they got Hank, the Ericksons got a St. Bernard puppy, which soon outgrew Hank, who weighs about one hundred and thirty pounds.

"Hank is not a dominant dog," explains Keri. "If I tell him, sit, he'll sit. I call him, he comes. The fact that he listens to me helped us train the puppy. The puppy is stubborn. He's also big and hard to handle. But he follows Hank's lead. When Hank sits, the puppy will sit. It made it a lot easier to train him."

Keri loves Hank, and he returns her devotion. One day, she was cleaning out a shed on their property. "It probably hadn't been cleaned in twenty years. I was up on the ladder, cleaning out wood and old guttering pieces, and came across a rat's nest. I gave out a healthy holler. Here comes Hank running into the shed. I got off the ladder and told him it was okay. He lay down for the rest of the afternoon in the door of the shed where he could keep an eye on me. He was guarding me.

"If we had any concerns about Hank being unnecessarily violent, his behavior in the last year has shown us that he can be trusted. More than that, he's a great protector and friend."

Hank has proved his tarnished reputation was undeserved and has secured his place in the Ericksons' hearts.

A Very Special Boo Boo

Every Wednesday, Christy Becnel (now O'Halloran) and Robin Pannagl, volunteers from the Southern Animal Foundation, went to the Plaquemines Parish Dog Pound to pull out potentially adoptable dogs who would otherwise be put to sleep the following day.

"The day we pulled Major from the shelter was a typical Wednesday," recalls Christy. "There were way too many dogs for us to take; we really didn't have the room because we foster them in our homes, but we had to pull them anyway. We knew that God would take care of us, and the pets we took would eventually find homes."

They had just finished pulling the ones they thought were adoptable when Christy looked through the outside door of a run and saw a group of mangy dogs they had missed.

"The first thing to catch my attention was a pair of eyes looking back at me," she says. "It was Major. He was skinny and missing a lot of hair, but I knew I had to take him. There was just something in those haunted gray eyes that beckoned me." He reminded her of her mother's dog, a Weimaraner. The dog was ten or so weeks old and had probably been picked up as a stray.

Major was too scared to come to Christy, so she got down on her hands and knees and crawled through the dog door to the interior part of the run. "I kept praying that the big dogs were nice and would not decide to pull me through the dog door as I poked my head through."

Christy managed to get him out in spite of his fear. She filled out the necessary paperwork and immediately took him to a veterinary clinic. "As soon as he came home with me, after being fixed and vaccinated, I gave him a good flea bath and dip. He gave me instant thanks with licks of love." She named the bluish silver Weimaraner mix Major, after her mother's dog, and posted his photo on Petfinder.com and hoped that someone would see what she had seen in him.

Amy Downey, who lived in Marrero, Louisiana, at the time, was looking at Petfinder.com and saw Major's photo. "I just have to have that dog," she told her husband, who replied, *"Absolutely not."* They had one four-year-old Jack Russell terrier mix named Marley they had adopted from a shelter when they lived in Ohio, and at the moment, they were bottle-feeding two kittens after animal control had picked up their mother at the factory where Amy worked but had left the babies.

"They didn't have their teeth, and their eyes weren't open yet, so the resident sucker took them home," she says of herself.

Amy begged Jason just to look at the photo of Major on the computer and, once he did, he agreed to go meet the pup. When they arrived at Christy's, Jason leaned over to greet the pitiful, emaciated dog with the protruding hipbones and ribs.

But then Major playfully jumped up on him and promptly relieved himself.

"Oh no, there goes any hope of adopting him," Amy thought. She was surprised when Jason said, "Yep, that's it. He's ours."

"My husband normally wouldn't put up with that, but there was something about Major."

There was indeed something special about him, but it would be over a year before they realized how fortuitous was the decision they'd just made.

When the Downeys adopted their terrier, Jason hadn't been too enthusiastic about adopting the dog, so Amy had named the pooch *Marley*, after the late reggae singer/songwriter Bob Marley, one of her husband's favorite artists, thinking it would win him over. One of the cats they'd bottle fed was named *Ziggy*, after one of Bob Marley's sons. To them, the name *Major* didn't fit their new pup, so they decided to rename him *Rohan*, after another of Marley's sons.

Rohan was scared of everything when they brought him home, Amy recalls. "Jason and I worked opposite shifts, so there was someone there with him all the time, and by the time he was six months old, he was afraid of nothing. He had lots of confidence."

He was also protective of Amy. They lived in a marginal area and "some guy was trying to walk up to me and talk to me—

maybe to ask for money," Amy relates. "Rohan jumped up and pinned him up against the wall of the house. He didn't try to bite him, just pinned him so he couldn't get any closer to me."

In August 2002, Rohan's allegiance changed. Amy and Jason had a baby girl, Noelle. "Rohan adored her from the moment we brought her home from the hospital. He slept under her crib," Amy says. She pauses as her next words catch in her throat. "I owe everything to that dog."

Noelle contracted pneumonia when she was three months old. "I had to sleep in her room and give her breathing treatments around the clock," says Amy. "One night, Rohan, as usual, was sleeping under her crib. I hadn't slept in three days. I was on the floor in her room and had finally fallen asleep. Rohan scratched my face. I looked at him and said, 'Rohan, you'd better go lie down; don't touch me. Lie down.' I was trying to whisper, but be stern at the same time. I had just fallen back asleep, and he scratched my face again. It was completely out of character for him. He's very well mannered. The second time he scratched me, I got up to put him out of her bedroom and noticed my daughter wasn't breathing."

Panic surged through Amy's heart. She quickly lifted the baby out of bed, and the very action was enough to start Noelle's breathing again.

Amy was beside herself, and it took some time to get her own heartbeat back to normal. Once she settled the baby in bed again, the grateful mom lavished hugs on the wonderful dog, who took it in stride but probably wondered why he was getting so much attention.

"Ever since, those two have a bond that is just amazing to watch," Amy explains. "When Noelle was first learning to walk, he would stand beside her and let her hold on so that she wouldn't fall over. Wherever he goes, she goes and vice versa. He still sleeps under her bed every night."

When Noelle began talking, she couldn't pronounce *Rohan*, so he got a new name. She called him *Boo Boo*, and soon Jason and Amy were calling him *Boo Boo*, as well.

"I knew the moment I saw him on Petfinder.com, he was supposed to be with us," Amy recalls. "I just didn't know why." That night in Noelle's nursery, and the countless nights since then that Rohan has watched over the little girl, proved beyond a shadow of a doubt that Boo Boo has a place in the Downey family.

Hello Dolly!

Someone tipped off the Humane Society of Union County in North Carolina that a person was operating a puppy mill out of an old barn. They launched an undercover investigation and presented their evidence to local authorities to secure a search and seizure order.

Cindy Poppino, president of the humane society, went along on the bust. When she entered the barn, the smell almost knocked her over. Before her were hundreds of small, wire-bottomed cages, perhaps two-by-two feet. Beneath them, the feces was piled up a foot or two deep. "I had never seen anything like it," she says.

The barn was bad enough, but the house was perhaps even worse. "You couldn't go in certain rooms," Cindy reports. "Feces and urine covered the floors, and newspaper had been layered on top of it. There were rubber tubs with dogs in them. It was brutal—much worse than we thought it would be."

They rescued two hundred fifty-seven dogs that day.

"We think the woman was forewarned and had relocated some of the breeding dogs and most of the puppies," Cindy says sadly.

The Humane Society and Animal Control of Union County assigned numbers to the dogs, crated them, and transported them to the animal control facility, where they had a veterinarian doing triage, pulling out the ones who needed emergency medical care first.

The humane society posted a plea for help on the Internet, and animal placement groups began taking the dogs.

Eventually, some of the dogs came to Christine Keller, the owner of Upper Chihuahua Rescue in Spartanburg, South Carolina, who fostered them in her home. One of these was Willow, an extremely shy, fawn-colored Chihuahua.

Christine posted Willow's photo on Petfinder.com, and an elderly husband and wife adopted her. It was a good placement for the little dog, but unfortunately it ended too soon when the wife died unexpectedly. The husband returned Willow to Christine.

The dog's shy demeanor didn't help her find another family. When people came to meet Christine's fosters, the other dogs were lively and vied for attention. Willow hung back. She was with Christine for a year while other dogs came and went.

Fate began to play its hand. In Fletcher, North Carolina, Amanda Surrett was about to celebrate her tenth birthday, and she wanted a dog. Her parents had given her the go-ahead.

She logged onto Petfinder.com and entered the keyword *Chihuahua*, the breed on which she'd set her mind, and up came a list of adoptable Chihuahuas. One dog stood out as Amanda browsed the list: Willow. "Her eyes were so sad," Amanda recalls.

She told her mom, Michelle, this was the dog she wanted, and Michelle spoke to Christine and arranged for the family to go to Spartanburg to meet Willow.

"We became more excited about our potential new 'child' as the miles clicked by," Michelle says. "When we arrived, we were welcomed into the home and suddenly were enveloped by barks, yaps, wagging tails, and jumping paws."

Amanda searched the room, trying to match up one of the eager dogs with the one she had seen on Petfinder.com, but it wasn't happening.

"After a few minutes, Christine brought her over to us," Michelle says. "Her eyes were large and she shook softly. Her tail was so tightly tucked I don't think you could have pried it lose with a crow bar. She made not one peep."

Michelle was having her doubts. She hadn't expected the dog to be so timid. Looking around at all the lively dogs, she asked her daughter, "Are you sure you aren't interested in one of the others?"

But Amanda wouldn't budge on her decision. She knew this was the dog for her. Her older sister, Camille, who was eleven at the time, agreed with her. They already loved this pooch.

Michelle finalized the adoption and headed back to North Carolina with Willow's food and a baby blanket she'd been sleeping with to make her feel comfortable.

But "comfortable" wasn't something Willow, renamed Dolly, came to easily. "She would carefully scout out the living room before entering," Michelle recounts, "and then scuttle from the edge of the couch to under the coffee table to behind a chair, where she would lie down and observe us quietly with those large eyes."

The Surretts took her on car rides, hoping Dolly would enjoy herself. It was hard to tell if she did or not, according to Michelle. "She was very careful about hiding her emotions. Even if something of obvious doggy interest would go by, she never barked, whined, or made any sound."

Michelle worried that they had made a mistake. She wondered if Dolly would ever warm up to them. Then one day there was a knock at the front door.

Bark, bark, bark!

The family looked at Dolly with astonishment. She had finally spoken!

The day was a turning point. "A little more ice melted every day after that, and she emerged sparkling," Michelle happily reports. "She now sleeps in bed with us, under the covers, of course. Her tail is held aloft, and wrestling is a common game between her and our other dog, a rat terrier pup named Teddy."

Dolly is always ready to go for rides with just a *"Dolly, let's go"* for an invitation. "She plants herself firmly in the driver's lap," says Michelle, "and happily navigates."

Michelle sent updates to Christine, who related that some animal placement people suggested that she not even bother trying to find Dolly a home, that she was unadoptable. Michelle told her how thankful she was that she had not listened to that pessimistic advice.

Cindy Poppino loves to hear stories like Dolly's and said that the majority of the dogs rescued from the puppy mill adapted and blossomed. "What makes me sad for those animals," she said, "is that we didn't get them out sooner."

"Dolly is the happiest little dog I have ever had the privilege of knowing," Michelle says enthusiastically, "and she's a joy to our family."

On the Job

Dayle Coutu of Colchester, Connecticut, didn't need a dog. She owned an animal placement group for cats; the name, *Keep Us Purring*, said it all. That didn't keep people from asking her to take dogs.

The first request came when a woman called her about kittens in a barn. When Dayle went to rescue them, she found a mom and eight pit-bull mixes in the barn as well.

"What are you going to do with these dogs?" she asked the woman.

"Oh, I have people who are going to take them," the woman replied.

Two weeks later the woman called Dayle and pleaded with her to take them. Soft-hearted Dayle couldn't say no.

Since she hadn't ever screened people for dog adoptions, she enlisted the aid of Hot Water Rescue, based in Connecticut, who listed them on Petfinder.com.

Meanwhile Gina Coangelo of New Britain, Connecticut, had recently lost a dog to old age and was on a quest for one to keep her Border collie/shepherd mix, Bosco, company. In the past, she had visited shelters in person to find canine companions, but this time she logged onto the Internet and came upon Petfinder.com. She connected with Hot Water Rescue, who had some Lab pups, but a volunteer told her about Dayle's puppies, and when Gina saw the pup that she would name Mira, it was love at first sight.

"It was the fifth or sixth dog I had placed," Dayle recalls, "and I cried. It was hard to give her up. But seeing Gina with the dog was one of those beautiful things that you don't get to see a lot; they just connected."

Gina stayed in touch with Dayle, and shortly afterwards, Dayle e-mailed her about some other dogs she had rescued. Gina sent the photos of the puppies to her fiancé, Michael Guarnieri, at his work. Independently, they picked one of them as their favorite.

Dayle wasn't sure they should depend upon a first impression from a photo, so on a Saturday, she brought several of the puppies over to meet the couple at the tanning salon/spa that Gina owns.

It was the end of the day, and Gina locked up and let the puppies play. The couple's initial reaction held true, and they decided to adopt the eight-week-old springer spaniel/shepherd pup. She was mostly black with a white stripe going down from her forehead to her nose. Her chest was white with black flecks, and her ears were floppy. Mike, a history buff, named the new addition to their family *Mauser*, the name of a German infantry rifle.

One of the nice things about Gina owning her business is that the dogs can go to the shop with her. She spends most of her time in a reception area at the front of the shop, usually alone, and they keep her company.

One day about six months after getting Mauser, Gina's car was in the shop, and her mother came by to take her to work. Gina didn't want to impose by bringing along the dogs, but her mom said it was okay.

Gina started to take Mira, but the dog was snoozing so peacefully that she passed over her and called for Mauser to come along.

At the shop, he settled in behind the reception counter while Gina worked. Around four o'clock, Gina noticed a man pacing the sidewalk in front of the shop. He wore a hooded sweatshirt pulled low over his brow so she couldn't really see his face.

But "it was daylight, so I didn't get worried," Gina says.

The man abruptly turned and came toward the glass front door of the shop. Simultaneously, Gina opened a Twinkie and put it on the counter. Mauser smelled it and stood up on his hind legs to check it out just as the man reached the door. The dog spotted the man, bolted out through the reception-area gate and lunged at the door, feet against the glass.

"He didn't bark, it was more like a frothy snarl," Gina recounts. She was alarmed at how sinister the dog sounded and went running over to the door. "The man was already walking away. He saw the dog and it was like, 'See ya.'"

Gina settled Mauser down and led him back to the reception area. The next thing she knew, seven police cars converged in the parking lot in front of her shop. Police officers came in and told her that the proprietor of the hair salon next door had just been robbed at gunpoint. They asked her if she had seen the perpetrator, and Gina described the incident at her door.

"Mauser wasn't too happy with the policemen either," says Gina, but she now had the gate to the reception area bolted so he was contained. "That's okay," one of them told her as she tried to quiet the dog. "He's just doing his job."

And quite a good job it was. "If it hadn't been for Mauser, standing his ground, protecting me with his life, it could have been me," Gina says gratefully. "He is truly my hero."

A Twinkie wouldn't do. Mauser enjoyed a thick filet mignon for supper that night. Doesn't a hero deserve at least that?

Orlando and Dawn

The brindle boxer mix in the framed photo in Lorri Hare's office doesn't look like a normal dog. His face is rather misshapen, and his long tongue hangs out of the corner of his mouth. His head cocks to one side quizzically. In spite of the jaunty argyle sweater he wears in the picture, no one would call him handsome.

Lorri is director of the Bowling Green-Warren County Humane Society in Kentucky, and the dog in the photo is just one of thousands that has gone through the shelter during her tenure there. What makes this guy so special that he warrants a framed photo, right alongside one of her own dog?

An animal control officer found Orlando wandering about in a marginal area of downtown Bowling Green. Most likely, a car had hit him because his jaw had been broken. The accident had happened weeks or even months earlier and his bones had healed—unfortunately, they healed in such a way as to make the jaw nonfunctional. His long tongue dangled out the side of his mouth. With it, he could scoop up water and food, which he swallowed whole because he couldn't chew.

He is the sort of dog that staff at overcrowded shelters put to sleep because of a negligible chance of being adopted, but that was not to be Orlando's fate simply because of his pleasant personality.

"He quickly won everyone over and became a shelter favorite," says Lorri. "He tried to get in our laps and lick us with that big ol' tongue."

Orlando's story went on the Humane Society's Petfinder.com Web site in hopes of garnering donations to pay for his veterinary care. People sent money from as far away as Georgia and New York.

"A dental specialist called from Tennessee," relates Lorri, "and offered to fix Orlando's mouth. It was a very generous offer, but unfortunately, after seeing the dog's X rays, he told us it would do more damage to fix it than to leave it."

Orlando lived at the shelter for over a month, and then a reporter wrote a story about him for the *Bowling Green Daily News*.

That, coupled with his story on Petfinder.com, brought "applications from all over," Lorri says, "but he needed a special home. We used veterinary references to see if an applicant's pets were spayed or neutered and whether their dog was on heartworm preventative. We made sure their pets' shots were up to date. We wanted Orlando to be an indoor dog, so we were holding out for that, too."

One day, Lorri received an e-mail from Dawn Cadwell in Grand Rapids, Michigan. Dawn's friend, Sandie Riendeau, had read about Orlando on Petfinder, and directed Dawn to Orlando's story.

Lorri interviewed Dawn and concluded that she would be a perfect placement for their special dog. It reassured Lorri that Dawn already had two rescue dogs. She had adopted Jake, a corgi/sheltie mix, after rescuers found him in an alley with his dead mother and two dead siblings. The family of Dawn's second dog, a beagle named Lucy, left her behind when they moved. The pooch had gone through several interim placements before finding a home with Dawn.

Sandie Riendeau is involved in animal rescue, so she arranged transport for Orlando. One person picked him up at the shelter and drove the first leg of the trip, and then transferred him to another driver. That leg took him to Indianapolis where Sandie lived at the time. Dawn left her home in Grand Rapids in her VW and rendezvoused with Sandie in Fort Wayne, Indiana.

Dawn brought her dogs along to meet their new "brother." On the way to his new home, Orlando kept trying to get into the front passenger seat of the small car, but that was Jake's customary place, and the seven-year-old dog was not about to give it up to this young whippersnapper.

"It was like two kids," Dawn recalls, but she understood that Jake had to let Orlando know who was top dog in the family. Once he had established that, the trip went fine.

Orlando might not have been top dog in the car, but his size gave him an edge when it came to sleeping arrangements.

"Jake used to sleep next to me on a pillow," says Dawn. "Orlando would get up on the bed and stand and look at him, like '*You need to get out of the way.*' If Jake was asleep, Orlando would look at me as if to say, 'Why isn't he moving?'" Eventually, Orlando prevailed, and Jake quit sleeping on the bed.

"Orlando's a little con artist," Dawn says with a chuckle. "Almost every day, he gets me up at six o'clock in the morning. I go to the door to let him out. I turn around, and he's not there. When I go back to my room, he has jumped on the bed and taken my spot."

She says the same thing happens when they watch television. "He'll be sitting next to me on the couch. When I get up and go to get a beverage, I come back and he's sitting in my place. Wherever I've been sitting, he wants to be sitting there."

Maybe the short-haired pooch is looking for the warmest spot around to combat the cold Michigan winters. Dawn had that in mind when she bought him the little argyle sweater he was wearing in the photo Lorri has in her office.

"Now when he sees his sweater," Dawn says, "he goes *crazy*. You'd think I was giving him a steak or something. He jumps and runs. He doesn't like me to take them off of him, but eventually they have to come off to be washed." Dawn is an avid knitter and plans to make more sweaters for Orlando.

"He turned out to be the most loving and affectionate dog," Dawn says. "People say he's lucky, but I'm the lucky one. He brightens each day."

When Orlando's story was no longer on the humane society's Web site, people wondered what had happened to him.

"I have never had so many people call to ask about a dog," Lorri says. "They called from all over Kentucky and Tennessee." She was happy to report that he had found a wonderful home.

Orlando's plight helped other rescued dogs. "We had money left over from all the donations," Lorri says, "and we called the donors to see what they wanted us to do with it. They said we could put it in our sick and injured dog fund."

With a catch in her voice, she adds, "You get attached to so many pets but certain ones like Orlando stay in your heart."

That's Scamp

Kids' movies aren't Jackie Pittenger's usual fare, but every scene with Nevins the dog in the Dr. Seuss movie, *The Cat in the Hat,* had her rapt attention. When Dakota Fanning, who played Sally, was holding the pooch, Jackie got a good look at him.

That is definitely Scamp, she thought.

A few months earlier Scamp, a Yorkie mix, had been running the streets of Austin, Texas, with little chance, it would seem, of becoming a Hollywood actor. For his own protection, animal control officers picked him up and took him to an animal shelter. They fully expected his owners to show up to claim him, but days passed and no one came looking for the little guy.

Yorkshire Terrier Rescue Network (YTRN) regularly checks shelters for just such foundlings and puts them in foster homes.

They found Scamp and placed him in a home with young children. Unfortunately, his lively personality soon proved too exuberant for the foster family

"He had springs on his feet," says Jackie, who was his subsequent foster "mom." After answering a plea for someone to take Scamp, she brought him home to Grand Prairie, Texas, where she lived.

He was quite a handful even for Jackie, who was used to Yorkies. He learned to get in her cabinets right away, and when she took him to a friend's for grooming, he escaped. The two women had only been in the fenced backyard for a few minutes when Jackie's attention strayed momentarily. *Presto*—he was gone. The gate was locked, so the two women ran through the house, out the front door, and through another locked gate. They saw the dog, running down the street lickety-tear, being pursued by two strangers. After retrieving him, Jackie and her friend searched the fence for holes, but there were none. The dog had either squeezed between the gate and the post or climbed the chain link fence. It remains a mystery.

Jackie had Scamp for about four weeks before she posted his photo on Petfinder.com. Several people called to inquire about him, and then his big break came. Cristie Miele, an animal trainer for Animal Actors of Hollywood, needed a dog—not just any dog, but one that looked like the Yorkie/Chihuahua mix named Bugsy that was playing Nevins. A team of look-alike dogs was employed in shooting the film, and one of the dogs didn't get along with the children. Cristie needed a replacement fast because filming was already underway. Somebody logged onto Petfinder.com, spotted Scamp, and told Cristie to take a look.

When she saw Scamp's picture, Cristie agreed that he was a double and called Jackie in Texas.

As with all her foster dogs, Jackie had become quite fond of Scamp, so Cristie had to reassure her that the dog would be living with the trainer herself, in a home, and that once the filming was over, Scamp would be her dog. In her heart, Jackie thought that a job would suit this high-energy canine, but she called the YTRN board to make sure acting was a suitable career.

"For a happy-go-lucky dog who loves to meet people, movie acting is a great life," Cristie explains. "Our dogs get to come to work with us."

The YTRN board agreed. "They said Scamp would have a good life," reports Jackie. Jackie also called Cristie's veterinarian, who told her that the well-respected trainer takes excellent care of her pets, as does the company for which she worked.

As soon as YTRN approved the adoption, a representative from Animal Actors of Hollywood flew to the Dallas/Ft. Worth Airport. Jackie and Scamp met her there. The dog, of course, had to be crated to fly back to California, and he didn't take well to the idea. The Animal Actors's rep and Jackie spent several hours in the airport, using treats to lure him into the crate. At last, they were off, and Scamp's career began. Jackie didn't see him again until she watched the movie.

Normally a dog would be in training before he actually went to work, but Scamp moved right into filming. Each day he had to go to "hair and makeup" to get Nevins's little topknot hairpiece applied. Then it had to be curled. He took to it like a pro.

A close look at Nevins in the beginning movie reveals a dog with buggy eyes: that is Bugsy. His name is listed in the film credits. Later in the movie, the eyes of the dog aren't quite so buggy: that is Scamp. Other than that, the two were quite a good match, enough to fool even the director. Sometimes during Scamp's scenes, he said, "Bugsy, open your eyes," not realizing it was Scamp.

"He's a pretty typical terrier with a bit of a stubborn streak, a 'what's in it for me?' attitude," Cristie says. "But he's very outgoing, and he was great with the kids."

And then it was a wrap, and Scamp went back to Cristie's to wait for his next assignment. Since then he has been in several commercials. Meanwhile in Texas, Jackie watched the movie: Conrad and Sally, going down a slide with the feisty little Yorkie mix, with his ponytail hairdo and perky ears. She smiled and thought to herself, *"That's Scamp."*

A Long Way Home

The person who had been feeding Bigfoot and his sister, Smiley, dropped the dogs off at the Humane Society of Putnam County in Greencastle, Indiana, when their owner had to go into a nursing home. In spite of losing their forever home, things were looking good for the dogs because the humane society staff chose them to take a ride on the CanINE Express from Indiana to New England, where less crowded shelters would give them a better chance of finding homes.

As the day of their big trip approached, the five shelters in southern Indiana that participate in the transport program prepared all the dogs. First, they were tested and vaccinated. Those that passed would be neutered or spayed before the trip. Smiley breezed through, but poor Bigfoot, a black husky mix with a tan muzzle and chest and short little legs, came up positive for heartworms. For him, the trip was off, and he had to watch as his longtime friend left for a new start.

Lainie Settecasi, a volunteer at the shelter, watched as Bigfoot slipped into depression at the loss of his companion. His physical condition didn't help. Lainie told her friend, Nancy Caraboa about his plight, and Nancy agreed to foster him while he received heartworm treatment.

Nancy works at the Indiana School for the Deaf, and she told another teacher, Kara Knebel, about Bigfoot. Heartworm treatment isn't cheap, and Kara's class, which had four children in it, decided to have a fundraiser to help pay for it. Lainie brought Bigfoot to the school to meet the children, and that made them even more determined to help the little fellow with a big smile on his fuzzy face. The kids made lemonade and cookies, sold the goodies in the cafeteria, and delivered two hundred dollars to the shelter.

The initial heartworm treatment made Bigfoot sick, and a vet tech, Jody Schemmerhorn, was there to comfort and help him. He then moved to Nancy's house, where she had to keep him quiet and calm during the remainder of the treatment.

Bigfoot became a trusted member of the family to everyone but Apollo, the Caraboas' Labrador retriever. He was jealous of the bond that formed between Bigfoot and the family's boxer, Roxy.

"If he had gotten along with Apollo, we might have kept him," Nancy says. Certainly the family cared enough for him. Nancy loved to hear Bigfoot and her daughter out in the backyard, Brittney singing and Bigfoot chiming in with a soft howl.

At last, Bigfoot's treatments ended, and the vet pronounced him well. As soon as he was neutered, he was ready for his second chance at a forever home.

Early one Thursday morning, Nancy took Bigfoot to a parking lot to meet Cathi Eagan, who founded CanINE Express and oversaw the monthly transport of about thirty Indiana dogs to the East Coast.

"They have done such a good job of spaying and neutering in the Northeast," Cathi explains, "that when I go up there, some of the shelters are virtually empty. They were looking for a source of good dogs."

Cathi loaded Bigfoot into her van, along with a letter addressed to "The lucky person who adopts Bigfoot." It ended by saying, "Oh, yeah, he smiles, too. Please let us know when you adopt him, so we can keep in touch." Nancy cried as she watched them drive away.

The transport made one stop in Batesville, Indiana, to pick up more dogs, and then it was on the road again. When the vans reached the eastern border of Ohio, it was time for a rest stop. The volunteers driving the vans took each dog for a walk. Then they headed into the long night, which ended with another rest stop as day broke.

"Friday was the day of delivery," Cathi recalls. She dropped Bigfoot at his prearranged destination: Baypath Humane Society in Hopkinton, Massachusetts, where the staff posted his photo and description on Petfinder.com.

In Ipswich, Massachusetts, Kelly Mastin was on a mission. She had a birthday coming up, and her boyfriend, Jeff Lebida, had decided the perfect present for her would be a dog. Kelly agreed. Both of them had dogs when they were growing up and had missed canine companionship.

"Kelly searched Petfinder.com every single day," Jeff says. "She came across Baypath Humane, which is about an hour and a half from where we live. It happened to be pretty close to Kelly's mom's house. We were going up there for Mother's Day, so we went by the shelter on the way." That was where they found Bigfoot.

"He was very cute and seemed friendly. He came up to the front of his cage and was looking at us, like *'Get me out of here.'*"

Kelly and Jeff responded to Bigfoot's eager look by taking him for a walk. "Once we did that, we were pretty set on him." The couple adopted the dog who had come so far to find them.

When Jeff read Nancy Caraboa's letter, he was amazed at all the people who had helped the dog get his second chance. He contacted Nancy, who was relieved to learn that Bigfoot had a permanent and loving home. The pooch had been through so much. It was nice to know that he finally had something to *really* smile about.

Fitting In

Sunny, an eleven-year-old yellow Labrador retriever, was not too happy about the new dog in his home. When she arrived, Sunny gave her a little curious sniff just to find out who she was, and she turned around, let out a growl, and bit him. After that, all Sunny wanted to do was avoid her.

The *idea* of a new friend wasn't a bad one. Sunny had been missing his companion, Hershey, who had died about a year earlier. Gradually, Sunny had filled the void left by Hershey's death, patrolling the perimeter of his property, looking out for squirrels and vermin. At night, he herded everyone to bed.

Now there was this new dog, and he didn't know what to make of her.

The new dog came from Montana, where her owners had reluctantly relinquished her to Pintler Pets, a humane society in Anaconda, for killing the neighbors' chickens. At first, her former owners would come and visit her at the shelter. However, when they left she cried, so eventually the staff asked them to stop visiting so she could better adjust.

Meanwhile, volunteers took her to adoption events and had her listed in the paper as The Pet of the Week. One month ticked by, then another and another. Though people inquired, no one stepped up to adopt Hopper, so named because of an astounding ability to spring straight up into the air.

Hopper ended up living at the shelter for eight months, and the folks there had about given up hope that anyone would ever adopt the chocolate brown dog who was listed on Petfinder.com as a German-short-haired pointer mix.

Then an e-mail arrived from Carol and Bill Campbell. "We live in Bellingham, Washington," it read, "and are interested in Hopper . . . We are prepared to drive to Montana to bring her home."

Later Carol said that the fact that Hopper had been in the shelter so long called to her. "We wanted to do the right thing and find a dog that was really in need."

The e-mail went on, asking questions about Hopper and telling the shelter staff about the Campbells' lifestyle. Not only was someone interested in Hopper, but if this adoption panned out, she would get to live with people who *truly* loved dogs. The couple lived adjacent to a park with lots of walking trails, they provided a variety of toys for their pets, and, in the past, they had adopted six needy dogs.

Phyllis Hargrave, a volunteer, said everyone at the shelter was ecstatic, as were many other people in town who had become acquainted with Hopper at adoption events. "They were all pulling for her."

The shelter approved the Campbells' application, and the couple made the long drive to Montana. After they picked Hopper up, they went to a campground in the area.

"We hadn't been there two hours when some people pulled in two campsites over with a couple of husky dogs," Carol relates. "Hopper immediately took exception to their presence and started barking and baying." All of the baying was enough to convince Carol that somewhere in Hopper's mix was some hound dog.

Once they got back to Washington, the dog gradually adjusted to home life rather than shelter existence. "She learned to be a pet," Carol says matter-of-factly. Along with Hopper's new start, the Campbells thought she deserved a prettier name, so they renamed her *Mocha*.

The Campbells were building a house, and Mocha loved to go to the job site, which is next to a state park.

"She barks at insects flying by and runs back and forth, nose down, following scent trails from nocturnal visitors, mostly mice and raccoons, sometimes deer," says Carol.

For Mocha, the world is a cafeteria of interesting smells.

Carol bought her a ten-pack of Frisbees, and the two of them play regularly. Mocha, with her built-in spring, is remarkable at Frisbee—every bit as talented as dogs on televisions, according to Carol. "Too bad I can't fling them well all the time, but Mocha is very patient with me when I throw one into the bushes."

The only thing that kept Mocha from being a perfect fit in the family was Sunny. The old boy just hadn't taken to the new addition after their first encounter.

Then one evening when it was time to go to bed, Carol called to Mocha, who was curled up on the sofa in the family room. The dog didn't budge.

"She'd had a busy day and was tired, so I didn't wake her," explains Carol.

Sunny assumed his usual responsibilities and herded Bill and Carol upstairs, and they got ready for bed. Customarily, as soon as the Campbells crawled under the covers, Sunny would settle down for the night in his own bed. Instead, he continued to wait by the door.

"He looked at me intently," Carol recalls, "wagging his tail—intent look, wagging, wagging. He seemed to be saying, 'Mom, Mom.' I finally said, 'Okay, what do you want?'"

Carol got up and went over to Sunny, who started down the hall. She followed. "Every time he turned a corner, he looked back to make sure I was coming." He led her down the stairs and into the family room and over to Mocha, who was still sleeping.

"*Get her up, get her up,*" Sunny seemed to say. But Mocha didn't want to get up.

Carol fetched a dog treat and, with that, lured Mocha up the stairs, Sunny right at their heels. Down the hall and into the bedroom.

Mocha lay down on her bed, munched her treat and settled in for the night. Carol climbed back into bed, exhausted and hoping Sunny was finally satisfied.

Sunny stayed alert until everyone was where they were supposed to be. Only then did he stretch out on his own bed with a sigh.

It was a turning point. Sunny had accepted Mocha as part of the family in need of herding.

All was right in both dogs' worlds.

A Fetching Fellow

The blind black-and-white cocker spaniel was waiting inside a crate that was much too small. It sat on the front steps of the owner's house when Zachary Williams, nine at the time, and his mother, Amy, drove up. They were responding to a plea from the dog's owner to come and get him because she didn't want him any longer. He was too much bother.

Zach, who is home schooled, had started a nonprofit organization, with his mother's help, to educate kids about pet care. It was called Parents Involved in Education (PIE) and provided a program to the elementary schools in the Palm Bay, Florida, area. Amy, Zach, and volunteers they enlisted held fundraisers and donated the money to animal welfare organizations.

It wasn't long, however, before people started dropping off their unwanted pets, hoping Zach would take them in. The first was a duck, Mr. Quackers, left under their information table at a fundraiser when he and his mom had stepped away. After several such incidents, the pair gave in and extended their mission to animal placement, calling themselves *Friendz for Life Sanctuary*.

Zach stepped around the crate on the front porch that held the cocker spaniel and knocked on the door. Moments later, the owner opened it, shoved out a bag with a few toys and medications for the dog's allergies, mumbled a thank you, and closed the door.

"She'd had the dog since he was a puppy," Zach says incredulously, "but she didn't shed a tear. She didn't even say goodbye."

The boy bent down and looked in the crate at the dog, whose name was Hunter. The most obvious thing about him was that he had been neglected.

"His hair was really long and matted, and he was full of fleas," Zach recalls.

Right away, Zach and his mom took the dog to the vet for vaccinations and neutering. Hunter was a purebred cocker, and the vet told the Williamses that the dog's blindness and his allergies probably stemmed from interbreeding.

Zach knew that cockers had a reputation for being nippy, so through all of this, he was truly expecting to be bitten. "Hunter was blind, he was taken from his home, he didn't know where he was going, he got neutered—and he didn't even bite us. He just loved us." Then and there, Zach re-evaluated his opinion of cocker spaniels.

"I made sure I played with him a lot because no dog should go through what he had." He also took Hunter to adoption events and listed him on Petfinder.com, hoping to find a permanent home for him. No one wanted a blind cocker spaniel with allergies, so Hunter continued to live with the Williams family for about two years.

Zach was surprised when he checked his e-mail one day and found a message from Susan Holstein in Indialantic, Florida, asking about Hunter.

Susan had owned an old blind cocker spaniel, Shelby, who had died. She also had a second cocker, twelve-year-old Casey. About eight months after Shelby's death, Susan read about Friendz for Life in the newspaper and decided to check out their Web site on Petfinder.com.

"I was curious to know what they were about and if they had any cocker spaniels," Susan says. They did, of course—Hunter. "I was just completely touched by his whole story."

The listing was very honest, relating all of the dog's health problems. Susan arranged to meet him at one of Friendz for Life's regular adoption days. The Williamses called Susan's references and did a home check. This looked like the perfect situation for Hunter, so they finalized the adoption.

"He wasn't very affectionate at first," Susan says, "but now I've got him giving me little kisses." She attributes Hunter's initial standoffishness to his health problems and his unfamiliarity with his new home. "I let him feel his way around the house, just making sure he didn't hurt himself. Since he was born blind, he didn't jump up on things. He stayed on the floor."

Gradually, Hunter became acclimated to his new surroundings. Susan took him for walks regularly and made sure he didn't step off a curb or bump into a tree. For the most part, she reports, no one notices that he's blind.

"There's a gentleman we met around the corner from us who gave Hunter some tennis balls," she relates. "Every time we go near that street, Hunter turns down there because he knows where the man lives. He makes a beeline toward the house to get a tennis ball. He's a smart little guy."

The tennis balls come in handy because fetch is his favorite game, a little unexpected for a blind dog.

"He can hear the ball on the tile floors," Susan says. "He runs down the hall, and he'll turn his head as if he's going to catch the ball. Once in a while he almost does."

One day, Susan had her friend's two dogs over for a visit. "They were sitting on the couch, and I had thrown the ball a few times and then quit paying attention," she says. Hunter wasn't ready to quit. He brought the ball over to the couch, put his front legs up on the cushions, and dropped it in front of the visiting dogs. "He didn't know who was there, but he knew someone was, and he wanted them to throw the ball again."

Susan's home is a good placement for Hunter, and from time to time, Zach sees the dog when Susan brings Hunter by an adoption event nearby.

"When Hunter left, my mom and I cried," says Zachary. "When you raise a pet from a baby or you've had them a long time, you get attached, but this is for the pets—not us, so you do what's best for them." As Zachary knows, best for Hunter is a "forever" home with Susan.

Problem Pet to Perfect

In a word, Mia was unruly. For one thing, the dog chewed everything she could get her mouth around. Amy Greene, her foster "mom," quit taking her to adoption events because she was so destructive. But how would Amy ever get this dog into a forever home if she couldn't take her to adoption days?

"Mia was my pick from the local shelter to foster," says Amy. "I thought she was a small golden retriever and I fell in love with her. But she had some *terrible* behavior issues."

Three months passed, and the dog's chewing was only getting worse. The Lake Area Partnership for Animal Welfare (LAPAW) in Lake Charles, Louisiana, that Amy fostered for called an emergency meeting about what to do with the pooch.

"That night someone in our group said she thought Mia might be a Nova Scotia duck tolling retriever," Amy recalls. "We looked up the breed, and glory be, Mia fit the description to a tee, including the destructive behavior if not regularly worked."

Amy contacted a Nova Scotia duck tolling retriever rescue group, sent them photos, and talked to them. They agreed that Mia was one.

"This gave us new hope for her. We knew what kind of home she needed."

A short time later, Amy registered LAPAW on Petfinder.com and entered Mia's information with specifics about the breed on the Web site. Her story jettisoned into cyberspace and landed on the monitor of the McLellan family in Vadnais Heights, Minnesota, when they did a search for a duck tolling retriever.

Months earlier, the McLellan kids, April, then twelve, and Keith, nine at the time, had expressed to their mom and dad that they wanted a dog. Gerbils, hermit crabs, cats, and a gecko had shared their home, but now they wanted a canine companion. Their parents, Anne and Rich McLellan, knew a dog would bring with it a lifestyle change for the family.

"The whole family sat down together and came up with a list of pros and cons," says Anne, "and what we thought would work for us. I didn't want them to think you just run out and get a dog impulsively."

The McLellans wanted a family-type dog, one that would get along with their other pets. They also decided to adopt a shelter dog because Anne felt people needed to take care of animals that already exist rather than encouraging more breeding. She started checking out humane societies to see what was available and also browsed the Internet. The family still hadn't settled on a breed when one day a new neighbor knocked on the McLellan's door.

"She had a dog with her," Anne recalls, "and as soon as I saw the dog's eyes, I knew this was the kind of dog we were looking for. It was one of those emotional things. She said it was a Nova Scotia duck tolling retriever."

Anne had never heard of the breed, so she began doing research on it. She read what little material she could find and visited retriever Web sites.

"Then I found Petfinder on the Internet," Anne says. "After about six or seven months of looking now and then, I started checking every day because I thought if one showed up on the Web, it would be snapped up quickly."

Her diligence paid off, and one day she saw Mia's listing. She e-mailed the foster family and shortly thereafter received a phone call from Allen Greene, Amy's husband.

Allen explained that a breeder had probably relinquished Mia to the shelter because she wasn't show quality, and then he told Anne about the dog's problem behaviors.

"I could tell he really wanted the right home for the dog," Anne remembers. "There had been another family interested, but it didn't seem right to the Greenes, so they were turned down. Fortunately, everyone who saw her fell in love with her and that's why she was kept alive at the shelter."

To the Greenes, the McLellans seemed to be a perfect fit. "They were an active family, who were always outside and wanted a dog to be with them on every adventure," says Amy. "I knew this was going to be Mia's 'forever' family." The only remaining hurdle was getting Mia from southern Louisiana to the McLellans' home north of St. Paul. Fortunately, the hurdle proved easy to scale, and on a January day, with the temperature hovering at ninety degrees in Louisiana, a professional pet transport company loaded Mia onto its truck and headed north to Minnesota. What should have been a three-day trip turned into almost a week, as the transporters ran into snowstorms. The one-year-old dog experienced snow and cold for the first time, and she arrived at the McLellans' door on a Wednesday evening with snow falling.

"We were heading off to a church function when they got here," Anne recalls. "They brought her to the door on a leash. We knew she had been through a lot, so I told the kids we had to be gentle and not overwhelm her."

The family decided to be a little late for church and sat quietly while Mia gathered her courage.

The McLellans had temporarily housed their cats in the bathroom, and they were introduced to Mia one at a time over the next several days. Mia and Smoky, a tiger cat they had rescued, hit it off right away. For Spice, a big fluffy four-year-old cat, getting acquainted was more problematic, but the two have learned to put up with each other.

"We did the best we could, prepared the best we could," Anne says, then adds with a chuckle, "but everything we did, we did wrong the first week. We were still reading the books. But she was just so loving. The Greenes did an incredible job with her. They had children and other pets, so she was well socialized."

The whole McLellan family went to obedience classes with Mia.

"I am the Alpha," Anne says, "but everyone in the family learned the commands. We absolutely fell in love with her."

The family gives Mia the activity she needs. Anne takes the dog on two walks or runs each day. After school the kids play with her, and in the evening, Mia accompanies Rich on a forty-five-minute walk. The McLellans live next to a wildlife preserve, so there are plenty of trails. Mia joins them on hikes, bike rides, and cross-country skiing jaunts. It's a good life for the former problem pooch, who is now a perfect pet.

On the Road Again

Lightning, thunder, dark of night—nothing kept Jackie Douglas from getting her pup. She'd spotted the little white furball, Cali, on Petfinder.com after her husband suggested a dog would keep her company when he went on the road. Scott Douglas is an off-road race driver, and Jackie usually travels with him, but not always.

The couple's race shop is in Little Chute, Wisconsin, and the pup was in Michigan. Normally, the two of them would have gone to meet her, but Scott had to go to Kansas to sign autographs when the couple's application to adopt was approved. He encouraged Jackie to make the trip to Michigan without him.

"I thought she was on the Upper Peninsula, about a three-hour drive," Jackie says.

It came as a shock when Scott pointed out that the dog was in Muskegon, Michigan, which is on the Lower Peninsula. Scott suggested, as a shortcut, Jackie drive to Manitowoc and catch the car ferry to Ludington, Michigan, which she did.

She spent the night in Ludington, and then started out again the next morning. Rain began to fall—not just a little spring shower, but a full-blown Midwestern thunderstorm. "It was the worst lightning and thunderstorm I've ever been in," Jackie recalls. "Cars and trucks, even semis, were pulling over."

Jackie stopped at a coffee shop to wait out the storm. She called the foster mom and said she was still on her way. The trip had become more trouble than she had expected. Finally, she pulled into the driveway at the pup's foster home. Out bounced the little ten-week-old Border collie mix. A brown spot surrounded one eye and her ears were tan.

"The moment I saw her I had no doubt that I was going to take her home with me," says Jackie.

The foster "mom" told Jackie that officers from Muskegon Vector Control had rescued the puppy from a freeway and had turned her over to Lifeline for Pound Buddies, an all-volunteer organization, which handles their adoptions. They, in turn, placed her in the foster home. Cali had been adopted once, but the family brought her back because she was too high energy for them. Not so for Jackie. The pooch was perfect.

On the ferry trip back to Wisconsin, Jackie rented a small stateroom for the four-hour crossing. Her intention was to smuggle Cali into the room so that the trip would be easier for the dog. But alert crew caught Jackie in the act and made her put the puppy back in the truck.

"The weather was cool enough," Jackie remembers, "but I felt sorry for her because she didn't know what was going on." Jackie could see the truck from her stateroom and kept an eye on it during the ferry ride.

The new "mom" had been thinking about names for the dog because, oddly enough, there was already a Cali in the family. Jackie and Scott had brought her parents a cat from California, which they had named Cali. So now Jackie had to come up with something else.

"People always say Scott and I are like peanut butter and jelly because we're together so much," and Jackie decided P.J. would be a cute name for the dog.

Once home, Scott began taking P.J. to the shop to let her become acclimated gradually to the noise of the trucks he raced. Within two weeks, it was time to hit the road to attend a Championship Off Road Racing (CORR) event. P.J.'s favorite spot turned out to be the passenger seat in their thirty-eight-foot motor home where she can survey the world as it rolls by. The puppy who was found on a highway now takes to the road quite a lot.

"She's a traveling dog," Jackie explains. "The motor home is diesel. When she hears a diesel engine, she gets excited. She's not going to be left behind. She also knows the words *motor home*."

The world of off-road racing is like a club. The drivers and their teams know each other and visit back and forth before and after races. It didn't take long before they all knew P.J. Some of the younger guys like to take her out on her leash, for more than one reason. "They say she's a chick magnet because all the girls come up and say she's so cute," says Jackie, laughing. "I buy her hot pink collars, and they're calling her Paris Hilton because all she does is prance around. She knows she's beautiful." And like Paris Hilton, she had become something of a celebrity.

"Scott was sitting at the autograph table, signing autographs, and P.J. was in the motor home because it was hot," Jackie relates. "Some people came down and said, 'Congratulations, Scott,' then 'Where's your dog? Where's P.J.?'" Jackie laughs. "They don't care about Scott anymore; they want to see P.J."

Scott takes this like any proud "dad." Sometimes, he even draws a paw print for someone and signs it *P.J.*

The dog loves the attention at the track, but she also loves relaxing at the Douglases' primary residence in El Cajon, California.

"She never has a bad day," Jackie says, "and when you've had a bad day, she's there for you." P.J. is a dog that was definitely worth the trip.

A Comforting Canine

The young paraplegic spent his days confined to bed or a wheelchair, unable to actively participate in his own life. But when Tia, a little white Australian cattle dog, bounced into his room one day, his eyes lit up and he started making kissing sounds with his lips.

His nurse expressed surprise. "He has never done anything like that before."

Since then, Tia and her "mom," Diana DiBello of Royersford, Pennsylvania, have made it a point to go to the young man's room first when they visit the rehab center, before Tia tires.

"Even though the man can't communicate, I can tell that Tia's visit is having a huge impact on him," Diana says proudly.

Diana had adopted Tia some months before without a single thought about her being a therapy dog. She was simply trying to fill a void left in her family by the death of her longtime companion cat.

She searched for some time on Petfinder.com before she located a dog she was interested in. Meanwhile, Diana applied for pre-screening at Hazleton Animal Shelter. Once the shelter approved the family's application, all that was left to do was to find the right pup.

When Diana spotted one she liked, she contacted the puppy's foster "mom," who suggested they set up a time for the whole family, including their six-year-old German shorthair, Cotti, to come and meet the puppy.

The foster home had two four-month-old female puppies to consider, a hard decision for the DiBellos. They sat on the living room floor and played with both pups, as well as the other foster and resident dogs in the home. The family brought in Cotti, who was no help. She loved all of them. After half an hour, Diana asked her husband what he thought. He cupped his hand under Tia's chin and said, "I think that you will be happier with this one."

Diana was delighted because Tia was indeed her favorite. With one blue eye and one brown one, the dog looked unique, and that appealed to her. "I was writing a check for the adoption fee before he could change his mind." The DiBello kids, Evan and Maria, loved their new family member, too.

Another reason the family wanted another dog was so Cotti would have someone to play with. "He was so needy," Diana says. "Now the two of them have a good time together. Cotti will bring a bone over and drop it in front of Tia. As soon as she goes for it, he grabs it and runs away. Tia herds Cotti all over the backyard.

If I call him and he doesn't come, she goes to get him and herds him into the house."

Cotti has become quite protective of Tia and barks at anyone who corrects Tia when she does something wrong.

About two months after adopting Tia, Diana had a jewelry party at her home. "I was more than happy to show off my dogs to the guests that had lingered after the demonstration," Diana says.

Her friend, Margie Alloway, who had done the demonstration and had been observing Tia all evening, asked if Diana had considered getting the dog into therapy work.

"I had heard of therapy dogs, but didn't know much about it," Diana admits.

Margie had two therapy dogs who worked with The Comforting Canines of Grace in Royersford, so she was able to fill Diana in on what was required.

Margie's words began to take root, and Diana decided to give it a try. Tia was only six months old at the time and had to be a year old to be certified, but Diana began training her right away.

"I pulled the certification test up on the Web and started training her for the specific things on the test," Diana says. Margie occasionally stopped by to check on the dog's progress. When Tia turned one, Diana applied for certification.

"A Therapy Dog, Inc., tester/observer put Tia through her paces," Diana explains. "She had to display appropriate behaviors in a number of situations, such as meeting people and other dogs. The dogs are also evaluated on appearance and tolerance to handling. The handlers are evaluated on their ability to control their dogs."

Observed visits came next. On their first such visit, Diana and Tia went to an assisted-living facility with other handlers and their dogs. The residents gathered in a day room where Tia showed off her first trick, waving her paw.

"I had seen this trick on a television show," Diana recounts. "I put a piece of tape on the side of her nose, and I would say, 'Cover,' and give her a treat. Eventually she was supposed to cover her eyes, but she never did that, so I changed the command to *wave.*"

Tia loved meeting the people, and they reacted warmly to her. Soon the pooch added new tricks to her repertoire, including rolling over and jumping through a hoop.

But most of all, people like to pet her. "Everyone comments on her fur," Diana says. "It's plush like a stuffed animal. The people who have arthritic hands stretch them out to feel her, and her head is the perfect height for someone in a wheelchair."

After Tia was certified, the pair began visiting care facilities with the Comforting Canines of Grace and another group, Karen's K-9, two or three times a month. She's always eager to go to work. When Tia sees Diana get her little training pouch and water bowl, she runs to the car.

Diana remembers one woman at one of the assisted-living centers who "was dressed perfectly, a matched outfit, hair nice, and her makeup on. She started petting Tia and said, 'You are doing me so much good,' and then she started crying. I talked to her a little bit and found that she had just lost her husband a week before. She was just devastated." The woman continued to cry, while petting Tia, who sat patiently, her head in the woman's lap.

"She kept apologizing for crying," Diana says, "but I didn't mind because I knew it was good for her to let it out. Every time I go to a nursing home or assisted-living facility, I leave feeling so good because Tia does so much good for the people there."

Melorah's Special Assistant

Jennifer McMahan looked in on her four-year-old daughter, Melorah. The little girl had been sick with what her doctor believed to be whooping cough, but she hadn't hospitalized her for fear that she might contract something else. The child had been physically vulnerable since birth, suffering from gastrointestinal problems, seizures, and developmental delays.

Now, Jennifer noticed how pale her daughter was. The worried mom wondered if the little girl was getting sick again. For Melorah, an illness could spiral downward quickly.

Jennifer reached out to feel her daughter's head and realized Melorah wasn't breathing. Immediately, the child gasped and took a breath. Melorah had another episode several days later. The severity of the incidents scared the McMahans enough to spur them into action.

"Melorah's neurologist had suggested that we get a service dog for seizure response," says Jennifer. "My husband and I spent hours on the Internet, looking at service dog organizations. Most of them would not place a dog with a child as young as Melorah. The few that would, required fees that ranged from $4,000 to $25,000 up front, and then there was a wait of two or three years. We didn't think we had that long."

Jennifer decided to go on to Plan B: get a likely dog and have it trained. When she spoke to trainers in the area, however, none was willing to take on the project, probably because while a dog can be trained to do many things, being alert to seizures seems to be a special sensitivity.

Jennifer wasn't ready to abandon her plan. "I thought, if nothing else, we would get a puppy, and it would bond with Melorah and help her socially, and then maybe we could figure out if we could train the seizure response." She began researching dogs on Petfinder.com, and one day she saw a listing for Castor.

Castor had been at the PAWS (Paris Animal Welfare Society) shelter in Paris, Kentucky, for five months. The staff had watched his enthusiasm wane as his days there accumulated. The Border collie mix used to jump excitedly when people approached, but he was beginning to lose the spring in his step. Though the shelter was crowded, the workers knew there was something special about this stray and didn't put him on death row.

Then Lori Woodward entered Castor's life. She had just moved to the area and volunteered to be a foster "mom." The PAWS staff asked her to foster Castor.

"He had no manners," Lori recalls, "so I started taking him to obedience classes with my other dog. Liz Norris, the trainer, evaluated him and said she thought he would be a good candidate for a therapy dog. We tested him with cats and children, and he did great."

Although Lori had fostered hundreds of dogs in the past, she had never fallen in to the "foster failure" category by keeping one. Castor, however, was working his way into her heart.

"Every time I took him to an adoption day," she says, "I ended up crying." She worried that he wouldn't get the special home he needed, one that would be stimulating enough for this lively dog. Each week when no one chose him, Lori was relieved.

"I had pretty much decided to keep him," Lori says, "and then I got a call from the shelter that a woman was inquiring about him." Again, fear gripped her. What if the caller wanted Castor? What if she wasn't good enough for him?

Jennifer McMahan had zeroed in on Castor's description on Petfinder.com because it said he might be a good service dog. When she got the call from Lori, the two women talked for over an hour. Lori felt relieved because Jennifer wasn't pushy about getting the dog. Instead, she explained Melorah's situation and let Lori know she was simply exploring the possibilities.

The conversation ended with plans for Jennifer and Melorah to drive to Frankfort to visit Castor during his obedience class.

By the appointed evening, however, Lori was again feeling anxious about losing Castor. "Jennifer brought some homemade dog biscuits," relates Lori, "and that worried me because I thought she would think she was taking Castor home that night. Then she handed them to me and said they were for my dogs. I was still defensive, thinking, *Just because you brought me a gift, doesn't mean he's yours."*

Then Melorah sat down with the dog, and watching them together, Lori's heart melted. During the class, Melorah drew a picture of Castor and wanted her mother to give it to Lori.

"Melorah, what is that?" Lori asked.

Melorah pointed to Castor.

Right then, Lori could see that the dog would be a way for the child to bridge to people.

"They took him home that night," says Lori, admitting that she cried every day for weeks after he left.

Jennifer was facing stresses of her own on the way home. "I prayed, *'Okay, God, close the door if this is not meant to be.'* I didn't want Melorah attached to the dog if it didn't work out, and my husband is not an animal person. I didn't want him to hate coming home from work each night." She knew, too, that her older daughter, Amelia, must not be allowed to bond with the dog if it was to be Melorah's service animal. That would be difficult because Amelia loved pets.

They got home about midnight, and put the dog in a crate in Melorah's room. Some time later, she heard him whimpering.

"I assumed he was just getting used to a new place, but I went in," Jennifer recalls. "Melorah was having a seizure. As soon as I went to her, the dog settled down and didn't make another peep." It was a brief seizure and abated quickly, and the rest of the night passed uneventfully. Jennifer thought it was just a fluke; she didn't even wake up her husband to tell him about the incident.

Two weeks later, she was up early and heard the dog whimpering again. She thought it was because he wanted out.

"I went in and Melorah was totally gray. She had stopped breathing. I roused her, but she didn't respond as quickly as she had in the past. If he hadn't whimpered, she wouldn't be alive today. I did wake my husband for that one. 'Do you know what that dog just did?' I asked him. 'He has earned his keep.'"

From that day on, Castor, now named *Hobo* because Melorah could say *Hobo*, went everywhere with them. He has been officially certified as a service dog, so he wears his service dog vest, which admits him to places other dogs aren't allowed. Jennifer continues to take classes to learn more about training.

It can still be difficult for his people to understand Hobo when he alerts them to danger. One evening, Hobo began knocking books off a shelf and then would run to Melorah. The odd behavior began again the next morning. Melorah was crying and holding her hand up to her head and saying, "water." Jennifer thought she was reacting to her hair being wet from a bath. Meanwhile, Hobo kept knocking the books off and running to Melorah.

Jennifer couldn't ignore Hobo's odd behavior and took Melorah to the doctor. It turned out that she had a major ear infection and Hobo was alerting Jennifer to it.

Another incident occurred in a restaurant. Jennifer had trained Hobo to sit quietly under the table at restaurants, and he did this very reliably. "This time he would not settle down. He kept standing up and sitting down and standing up. He was really restless." Jennifer was quick to blame herself for the dog's behavior. "I thought I wasn't giving the command right. But then half an hour later, Melorah had a seizure."

Jennifer says that everything has fallen into place with Hobo. "Our dog Millie loves him, my husband adores him, he loves the kids, and he alerts on Melorah. Hobo is a blessing." Hobo, too, is blessed by having found a loving family.

The Sweetness of Being

The seven-week-old puppy was crying and disoriented when the couple came upon her, but she didn't run from them or even seem to notice their approach. Soon they realized why: the little dog was deaf and blind. She was also adorable—a fuzzy little white baby with gray-and-orange patches and floppy ears—and petrified with fear.

The people scooped her up, and she eventually ended up at Aussielads Aussie Rescue in Mesa, Arizona. They'd seen pups like this, time and time again. She was the result of a backyard breeder's mating two merle-colored Australian shepherds, a pairing that results in genetic defects. Aussielads' mission is to educate people about the unfortunate practice that leads to affected puppies being culled and destroyed or abandoned like this one.

Finding good placements for normal dogs is hard enough. Finding suitable homes for ones with disabilities is even tougher. Aussilads took on the challenge.

Caitlin Gannon of Tucson was browsing on Petfinder.com, looking for an Australian shepherd to adopt. She and her partner, Teresa Terry, already had Blue, an aging Aussie, but Caitlin wanted a puppy. When she came upon the little rescued pup's photo, she picked up the phone and called Teresa, who was at work.

"You *have* to look at this dog," she told her.

"You could tell from the picture," Teresa reports, "that she was going to be astonishing."

When Teresa got home, they talked about the ramifications of adopting a dog with disabilities. "I have twenty years' experience working in children's mental health care," she says, "so I have extensive knowledge of behavior management. I thought if I could handle that, I could surely handle a disabled dog."

Despite Teresa's useful experience, they didn't make the decision lightly. First, they did research so they would know what they were getting into. Dire predictions of deaf and blind dogs being untrainable to snippy to hypersensitive abounded. In spite of those, they decided to proceed. Aussilads screened and approved their application, and Teresa and Caitlin brought the new addition home. They named her *Dolcezza*, Italian for "sweetness."

Although many of the things they'd read weren't true of Dolcezza, the first year was difficult. "She had a significant amount of anxiety," recalls Teresa. "She would twirl in circles and bark and bark and bark. It was a 'where in the world am I?' kind of bark. Sometimes we thought she was having a seizure. It would happen several times a day, and she was almost inconsolable."

They sought out people with similar experiences and, on their advice, tried various remedies. "A trainer astutely interpreted one of the issues as her not being aware of her body—always being in her head," Teresa recounts. "The trainer taught us to hold her when she freaked out like that until we regained control *for* her. 'Cezza originally didn't want to be held, but we did it anyway."

Meanwhile, when she wasn't out of control, she had the sweetest temperament in the world—almost ethereal, according to Teresa.

"We handled her firmly from the beginning so she would have a sense of place and being touched and being directed. And we must have done that right because now anyone can walk up to her and touch her, and she is okay with it. We don't worry about her biting people," Teresa says.

To see Dolcezza move about in her world suggests that her guardians did indeed do something right. She has confidence that belies her blindness. When they first took her to the dog beach in San Diego, she ran right into the water, chest deep and seemed to say, "This is the coolest thing I've ever felt."

Living with a blind and deaf dog put Teresa and Caitlin into permanent problem-solving mode. They used touch to teach her simple commands—followed by a treat, of course. House training went smoothly, but knowing when she needed to go out was a challenge initially. She would stand at the door, obviously wanting to go out, but because it wasn't really a door to her, just a location in the room, she didn't know to scratch. There needed to be a signal. The solution was to hang bells on the door at Dolcezza's chest level. When she approached the door, she ran into them, signaling her need.

Maturity has resolved many of Dolcezza's anxiety issues. Teresa draws a parallel to children who have problems with self-control. "They do mature," she explains, "and given good guidance, they learn self-control by virtue of maturity."

Teresa also attributes the change in Dolcezza to their adoption of another pooch—Amadeo, a nine-week-old Aussie who was sighted, but deaf. Their other dog, Blue, as it turns out, hasn't been much of a companion for Dolcezza. "She's mostly old and cranky," Teresa says.

Dolcezza and Amadeo became great buddies, running and wrestling all over the yard. In the midst of their play, Dolcezza would sometimes stop and return to the sidewalk to reorient herself. "You can see her mapping out where she goes," Teresa explains. "People will walk past the yard when the dogs are playing, and they can't take their eyes off of her. They think she's odd, but they don't realize she's blind. Her behavior is what they notice—and the fact that she is stunningly beautiful."

Caitlin and Teresa developed a Web site for Dolcezza. On it, they tell what they've learned about living with a deaf and blind dog and include many photos and videos of the dogs.

"We hear from people all over the world," reports Teresa. Some of them have special needs dogs, but others wonder whether they should adopt one. "I wouldn't recommend it to everyone. I tell them it's going to be work. At times, it was difficult and heartbreaking, and you have to have the patience of Job."

But Teresa and Caitlin would do it again in a heartbeat. "Dolcezza has a magical effect on people," Teresa says. "They can see that a dog with the severe impairments she has can have a ninety-nine percent normal life. Her tenacity and fearlessness are an inspiration. I wouldn't trade her for any animal on earth."

For the Love of a Schnauzer

When Lori Wilson's dog, Pepper, died, it was like the end of the world to her. "We had gone through lots of hard times together," the Winston-Salem, North Carolina, resident says. She couldn't shake the sadness, and eventually her husband, Troy, insisted that they get another dog to fill the void.

"I wasn't sure I could ever love another animal as much as I loved Pepper," Lori says, "but I did go on Petfinder.com. I was really fond of schnauzers, so I looked at the miniature schnauzers in my area. That's when I discovered Schnauzer Rescue of the Carolinas. I wasn't sure I was ready to adopt another fur baby or let another one into my heart yet, but I agreed to be a foster mom." For Lori, fostering was a way to give herself more time to heal.

One day she got a call from the rescue that a stray senior schnauzer they named Jordan needed a place to stay. Lori had seen Jordan's photo on Petfinder, and she agreed to foster him until the rescue could find a permanent placement for him.

The rescue took care of Jordan's immediate medical needs, including neutering and the removal of his top front teeth and a growth on his eyelid. They cleaned the dog up so he looked like a self-respecting schnauzer and transported him as far as Concord, North Carolina, where Lori met them and got a first look at her new charge.

"His eyes were cloudy with cataracts; he was partially deaf and his hip was out of alignment, which caused him to drag one of his hind legs," Lori recalls. "My first reaction was pity. I thought, '*No one* is going to adopt this poor old dog.' On the ride home, he explored my van and ate treats. He stayed in the floorboard because he was unable to jump up on his own onto one of the car seats. I also found out he wasn't completely house trained."

Lori had no intention of keeping Jordan, and her husband didn't want them to adopt an old dog for fear that they would go through the heartbreak of losing a pet again.

Jordan had other ideas…

That night, Lori put the dog bed she'd bought for him beside their bed, thinking he would want to be close to them. As soon as they had turned out the light, he stood beside the bed and began barking.

"I looked over at him," Lori says, "and every time he barked, his front feet came off the ground. I got so tickled. I asked him what he wanted, and he pawed at the side of the bed. I picked up the little rascal, and he began sleeping on the foot of our bed."

First into bed, then into their hearts. In April, Lori told her husband she wanted to keep Jordan; Troy was reluctant. "Let's make a deal," he said. "Let's also get a one-or two-year-old dog." A young dog would provide a little insurance against another devastating heartbreak.

Lori fully understood. "It has to be a schnauzer," she replied.

Thus, Julie came to live with the Wilsons. Later they adopted a third schnauzer, Jasmine.

Time and experience had taken its toll on Jordan's body, but his spirit was young. "He gets really excited when we come home, and he can't really run because of his back leg, so he hops around the house. He gets into everything just like a puppy."

Jordy loved to grab a roll of toilet paper and take off with his characteristic hopping. "If you ever see a woman chasing a schnauzer that hops, it just might be me," Lori says with a chuckle.

"I don't know how many years Jordy will be with us," Lori says, "but every day he gives us all he has. He's got a huge will to survive and enjoys life against all odds."

Perhaps the biggest impact Jordy had on Lori's life was that he inspired her to become an active member of Schnauzer Rescue of the Carolinas. She has fostered more than ten other schnauzers and has taken part in twenty or thirty transports of dogs to new homes.

"Maybe Pepper had to go because these other dogs needed me now," she says pensively. "Adopting Jordy opened up a whole new world to me."

Gift of Life

Kevin and Chelli Treat of Corning, New York, had hit rock bottom. "We had been through every unimaginable hell a person can experience in three years time," Chelli says.

It started when Kevin's parents passed away within weeks of each other, after long battles with lung disease. Then his uncle died, followed by his grandfather a short while later.

All of the losses in quick succession left the Treats examining their own mortality, and they realized what they wanted more than anything was to be parents.

They had already learned that they couldn't have children, so they decided to adopt. "We started with a private adoption," Chelli explains, "but when we went to the hospital to be present for the birth of our son, we were told that the woman we were dealing with was a con artist."

The private adoption fell through, so after overcoming their disappointment, the Treats applied to adopt through county services. After going through all the scrutiny necessary to adopt, their application was approved.

One day in October, their long-awaited dream came true, and a beautiful little girl came to live with them. Within a few days, their dream vanished when the child's grandmother filed for custody, and it was granted. They were given less than two hours to say goodbye.

"We were shattered," Chelli recalls sadly.

A week later, the Treats got a call that turned their lives around once again. The state had taken a five-day-old baby from her home, and the social workers wanted to know if the couple would take her in.

"It was going to be much different than we had dreamed," Chelli says, "because she was coming to us first as a foster child for at least a year." But that was okay with them. Chelli and Kevin were eager to start their family, and they were told that at the end of the year they could adopt her.

"Our life revolved around Carrie," says Chelli. "We never thought of her as a foster child. We loved her as if she were our own."

The idyll ended on March 7 when Carrie died in her crib, probably a victim of Sudden Infant Death Syndrome (SIDS).

"There are truly no words for what we felt at that time," Chelli recalls, her voice choked. "We continued to breathe in and out, but our emotions and senses had shut down. We felt as if we died in that crib, too. We'll never be the people we were."

In July, a brief ray of hope emerged when the state placed a two-year-old boy with the Treats for eleven days. "It looked really good, and they said we would be able to adopt him," Chelli said. "Then somebody realized that he shouldn't have been put with us because the cause of Carrie's death had not been determined. We were on hold."

By September, the Treats were only going through the motions of living, and Chelli knew it was critical that they find a way to put some meaning back in their lives. She began browsing on Petfinder. com, a site she had visited before when she had considered getting a companion for the couple's Jack Russell terrier, Scooby. "Feelings that I thought were gone forever were coming to the surface as I read the pet descriptions." That evening, she talked to Kevin about adopting a dog, and he agreed that it would be a good idea.

One of the first dogs Chelli saw on Petfinder.com was at Mini Mutts Rescue in Painesville, Ohio, so she searched their list. The Treats filled out an application and e-mailed it to Carla Nelson, the owner of Mini Mutts.

Carla responded to their e-mail, telling them that the dog they were interested in was already promised to someone else. But she had another dog that matched what they were looking for. She took some photos during her lunch hour to send to them, something that Chelli thought was particularly special. It made her feel she was almost seeing the dog in real time.

The dog, Marla, a tri-colored toy fox terrier mix, "stole my heart the minute I opened the first picture," says Chelli. By the next morning, their application to adopt Marla had been approved.

Animal control had picked Marla up as a stray, and the chaos at the shelter had sent her cowering into a corner of her crate, growling. At an overcrowded shelter, "they were not going to waste time finding a home for a dog like her when they have bouncy little puppies," Carla explains. Fortunately, they called Mini Mutts. "We took her in a heartbeat." Once Marla was out of the shelter, she no longer was aggressive.

On a September morning, Chelli, Kevin, and Scooby piled into their Jeep and headed to Erie, Pennsylvania, where Carla agreed to meet them.

"We arranged to meet at a Cracker Barrel on the Interstate," Chelli recalls. "We were early. There was a grassy area nearby, and we stopped there to let Scooby out."

Chelli began to worry. What if Carla didn't show up? They'd had so many disappointments.

To ease her anxiety, Kevin suggested they take a drive.

"*No,*" Chelli said firmly. "We might get a flat tire and miss them." She was so afraid something was going to go wrong.

Finally, Chelli saw the car come around the corner, and relief flooded over her.

Carla recalls, "As I drove up, Kevin was snapping pictures, just like a parent, and Chelli was crying."

"Here comes our little girl," Chelli told Kevin.

The dog was standing on Carla's lap, looking out the window when the car pulled to a stop. Carla opened the door and before she even got her feet out of the car, Marla went right into Chelli's arms.

"She was such a peanut," Chelli remembers fondly. "I couldn't believe how small she was."

The new "mom" was overcome with joy. "She was really there and no one could take her away. It was all happening for us."

It was even happening for Scooby. He and Marla bonded immediately and snuggled up on the backseat for the ride home.

For Chelli and Kevin, the new member of the family was a miracle. "Marla was a gift we needed so desperately. We gave each other a second chance at life."